ℳetamorphosis

"Inspirational stories of women living with Alopecia"

TO:

_____

FROM:

_____

DATE

_____

SPECIAL MESSAGE:

_____

_____

_____

_____

✒Metamorphosis

"Inspirational stories of women living with Alopecia"

Embrace *Change*

Julia L. Crittendon

$\mathcal{I}$ncomplete

I was a paralyzed spirit, enraged by the growing numbness I did not feel,
as it surpassed consciousness and then filtered down through my body.
My heart, immune now, never was bold enough to become numb, and,
I will embrace the rhythm that the breath of life marches to since,
Without it, certainly, I am incomplete.

I am Intrigued by time, its uncertainties, and how it heals emotional wounds,
But refuses to abolish the emotional memories.
Though unsure of the stipulations of time, the one certainty,
Is that 'my' time is not infinite, I will cherish and love it.
I should…I must remind myself to breathe slow.

I am fascinated by beauty, though it is delivered from misconception,
The most attractive face is no exclusion to life's protocols.
But, beautiful minds are blessed with wisdom, a miracle alone;
While intellect often becomes plagued by insecurities,
I will never hinder my stride to conquer.

I am inspired; God, grant me the serenity to be an inspiration,
To captivate the one who remains still, but still waits to be moved.
To encourage the one who is inspired, yet unmotivated!
I pray that my faith never diminishes.
Without it, certainly, I am incomplete.
--Tonya Stone

$\mathcal{D}$edication

It's been a journey to say the least and my husband who's my rock has given me an over abundance of Love, Patience, Strength and most of all Acceptance. I could not imagine my life without him in it. He saw in me what I couldn't see in myself, true beauty! I thank him for not turning his back and walking away but for staying and helping me find ME.

My three Angels for being so well behaved and AWESOME kids.

Finally to all Alopecians, we need to wake up societal standards. Come out of hiding and help educate and raise awareness about this condition called Alopecia. It's not going anywhere but we must LIVE life. I challenge you to LIVE!

Where there is awareness and education, there is understanding!

LOVE SELF…

$\mathscr{A}$cknowledgments

God has been the light unto my feet on this path. I thank God for supplying all of my resources.

This project would not have been a success without the women and children involved. They stepped out of their comfort zones to show the world just how beautiful "bald" is. We didn't ask for this to happen to us, it just did and it showed up in our lives for a reason. I'm just glad that each of you showed up in a way that will help others deal with the affects of being bald in this world of ours.

The photographers and poets who donated their time and energy to this cause, your work is beautiful, thank you.

To LIFE there is purpose why you do what you do. Now it's up to each one of us to find out what that purpose is and embrace it.

Thank you!

Table of Contents

Unfolding
(Butterfly Stage)
"Song of the Strong" by D.R. Hill

New Blooms
"Learning How to Fly" by Carol Jones

Metamorphasis Final Thought

OREWORD

My name is Carri and I am a 36 year old wife, mother and daughter who was diagnosed with Alopecia Areata on February 14, 2008.

When I was asked to write my story I didn't feel like I had a story to tell because to me a story has a beginning, a middle, and an end. How can I have a story in just five months from being diagnosed? I feel I am still so in the beginning that there is not a middle or end in sight. I am no where near being able to understand why this is happening to me. I am still trying to wrap my new hairless head around everything that has happened. Yes, I understand the medical part that my white cells are fighting my hair follicles but I don't understand why it has taken such an emotional toll on me. I have this new thing I have to deal with daily that is obviously not going away anytime soon.

My entire life has revolved around my hair. From the day I was born I have been the red haired, fair skinned, freckled girl. It only became cool to be me when the movie Annie came out when I was ten years old. I hated my hair as a child because it gave kids fuel to call me names.

I will never forget one instance in elementary school when two boys were making fun of me at the bus stop. I ran home crying to my dad who proceeded to walk with me back to the bus stop. He gave the two boys a chewing out and they never bothered me again. I have always hated attention being drawn to me. I hated it then and I hate it now.

I now look like the woman on chemo. People always assume you have cancer when you do not have any hair. I get the stares and the look of sympathy. I already know what they are thinking "Oh that poor woman with cancer and look she has a daughter". My husband and I were in a restaurant a few months ago and a lady came right up to our table when we were eating and asked me if I had cancer. I don't think people mean to stare but it is human nature to look at the different one.

I have two wigs but I have burnt both of them with steam from the oven. It serves me right; see cooking is bad for your health or at least your wigs. It actually frizzes them right up. I did it once without knowing the consequences and the second time I did it because I was just in a hurry to get dinner ready for my family. The new life comes with new things that you have to think about.

We went to the beach a few months ago and I panicked for weeks before wondering what I was going to do. I can't show my bald head to the world on the beach. I ended up wearing a baseball hat in the ocean and it turned out fine.

There are things that I worry about now that I never would have given a second thought to before. I hate having to deal with all of this. I don't want to be different. I don't want to live life on the sidelines! I want to participate in the game. Don't get me wrong I am grateful that I do not have cancer but I am aggravated in the annoyance of this disorder. There is basically no treatment. You just sit around and wait to see what happens next.

I don't know when the middle or the end of my Alopecia will be here. I guess one morning I will wake up and say today is the day I feel more comfortable with all of this... I just have to take one day at a time. I don't know if I will ever have the confidence to walk down the street without something on my head. I feel naked without hair and I think society puts pressure on us to be perfect and to have perfect hair.

I just need to remember that God thinks I am perfect in his eyes no matter what the world says. Philippians 4:13 says "I can do everything through Him who gives me strength". I do feel that things happen for a reason and obviously I have been blessed with this disorder for a greater purpose then I can see right now. It is easy to get caught in your own pity and not venture out of your own circle but I know that I have to find peace somewhere along this road. I will survive this and hopefully come out a better and stronger person. God Bless.

$\mathcal{I}$ntroduction

"Scotlyn was 6 months when I started loosing my hair."

I used to always play in my moms hair. I'd imagine that I was washing her hair and blowing it dry. I'd usually put it on some curlers or put braids in it. Majority of the time my mom would want me to scratch her scalp for dandruff, she would usually fall asleep when I started scratching it.

The one incident that brings back memories is when I got the comb stuck in her hair. See I just imagine that the comb was a curling iron. So I twirled the comb around and around until I thought the curl was tight enough. I held it there, barely touching it as if it was hot, watching the imaginary steam coming from the comb. See, I remember taking this all in watching my mom as she would curl her own hair.

Well it was time to take out the curling iron, I mean comb.

"Oops!" I said.

"What are you doing to my hair?" my mom asked me as she was feeling around in her hair.

"Lynann!!" she yelled. Lynann is my middle name, and I knew right away that I was in trouble.

"Why did you do this?" she asked.

"I was just making your hair pretty." I said

She was so upset with me. It took her such a long time to actually get the comb untangled from her hair. Even though she was upset that never stopped her from letting me do her hair, she would just be more aware of what I was doing to her hair from that point on.

I shared this story because when I was pregnant with my little girl Scotlyn, I couldn't wait until the day she got into my hair. I knew from experience that there would be so much imagination and creativity on her part. I wanted to see if she did the same things as I did with my mother.

Scotlyn was 6 months old when I started loosing my hair. As the months kept passing and with every new spot I found in my head the vision of her ever doing my hair was fading. By her first birthday, I was completely bald.

I look back at those moments of depression and the questions of "why is this happening to me?" I'd lost such a huge part of what I thought made me, me.
I felt so ugly, therefore looking in the mirror was not an option. However, one day my husband caught me taking a glance in the mirror. I just started crying.

"I look like some sort of creature", I yelled.

"Are you going to leave me?" I asked him.

They say that love is blind and clearly he could see this horrible thing that was happening to me.

"J, I didn't marry you for your hair", he said

"I married you for the person you are on the inside, your beautiful personality."

"You're beautiful to me even without hair", he said

I just cried and hugged him so tight, I didn't want to let go.

I recall speaking to my mom on the phone that same week. I had just gotten my test results back from the Endocrinologist. I told her that the test came back normal.

"I'm not dying mom", I said.

"Be patient Julia, and try not to look at patience as a bad thing", she said softly.

She didn't elaborate on that statement and I just said "ok".

I figured it out later on what she meant, the revelation would come to me after 2 bouts of remission each followed by hair loss again. She wasn't so much speaking about my hair coming back, not as much as she wanted me to take the whole experience in, trust God, grow, learn and continue living.

So it hit me and I had this AWESOME stance on my life which was finding out who Julia was and to ultimately love myself totally. Thus my journey to "me" started.

Everyday I find something new that I appreciate about myself and everyday I thank God for the strength that He gives me to keep on moving toward my true purpose.

Julia L Crittendon
Alopecia Areata since 2002

"Everyday I find something new that I appreciate..."

A "Metamorphosis"
definition when it comes to Alopecia

A physical, mental and emotional transformation

An abrupt change

A change in appearance

A change done in stages

$\mathcal{M}$etamorphosis

"Inspirational stories of women living with Alopecia"

The concept of the book derived from my own experience from living with alopecia, also from hearing stories from other women and their walk with this deficiency. I found that everyone's story is similar from a medical stand point, but emotionally we were at different points in our lives when it came to how we felt about "self".

When I think of Metamorphosis, I think of a complete change in physical form and emotional form when it comes to alopecia.

The cycle begins just like the female butterfly who ventures out to find a hosting plant to lay her eggs. As a person with alopecia at this stage, the egg stage is in which one is new to what's happening to them, they just want to understand. Therefore they venture out to find resources and answers to what is happening to them. It's hard at this stage because we have such high hopes that this will pass and that the "normal" life we use to live will resume soon. Denial sets in and we usually refuse to believe that this is going to a part of our lives. Wigs and head coverings become a large part of who we are becoming so we won't loose the sense of who we were. At this stage we still continue to stay focused on the "The Surface" (I just want my hair back, stage), nothing else matters at this point.

As the egg hatches and the caterpillar (larva) emerge, a new adventure begins. At the Larva stage, one starts to show signs of change in their physical appearance and "Growth" in their attitude. They are still trying to understand what's happening to their body.

The caterpillar then starts to feed on plants so it can grow. Then the skin on the caterpillar becomes too small and the old skin opens so the caterpillar can come out with new skin. This will happen several times as the caterpillar continues to eat and grow. Once the caterpillar is fully mature, it makes a silk pad on a leaf, attaches itself to it and prepares for the transition. At the Pupa stage, one starts to realize that they've grown. "The Transition" is where one becomes more prominent in their skin. They no longer let comments bother them and they start to have a strong sense of self.

When one starts the "Unfolding" process at the Butterfly stage, they start to display a sense of self awareness. This change is now a way of living that will not run their life, just simply be a part of it.

The women featured actually reflect each one of the stages mentioned. However, the stories that they share are better suited for the stage that they were placed in throughout this book. The hope is that their experience will somehow help another woman understand, heal and move on to the next stage, ultimately finding peace within her.

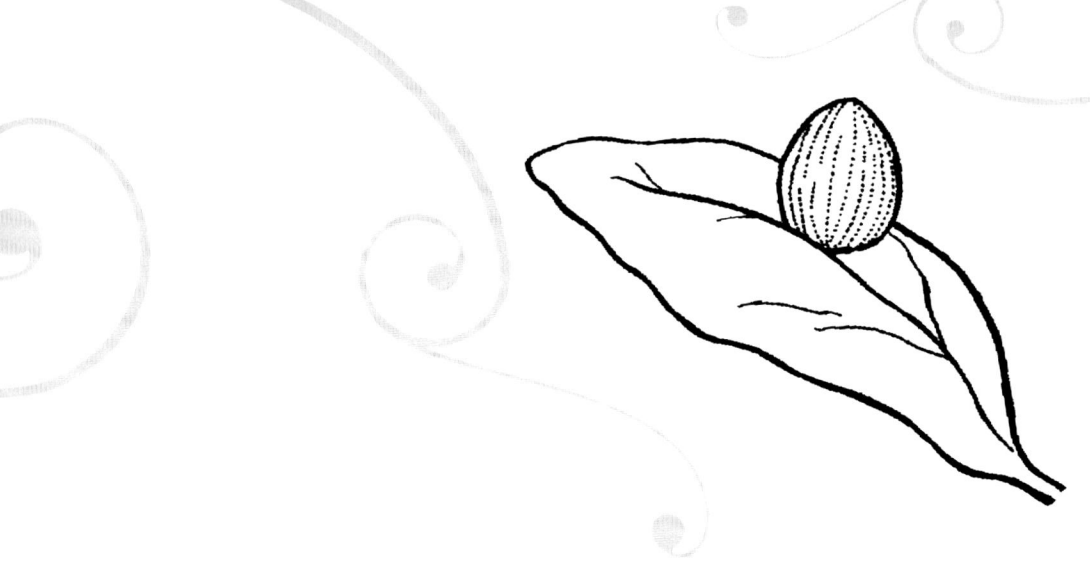

The Surface

(Egg Stage)

"When I look back at my life I think to myself, "How in the world did I get here?" Never did I think that I would have this type of change in my life. Having kids, yes, gaining some weight, yes again, but whoever thinks about being bald one day. I certainly didn't!"

Julia Crittendon

y Truth

Mirrors show reflections
Reflections show truth
When I look into the mirror I see my truth

What is my truth?
Immeasurable, inexplicable beauty
A beauty beyond descriptions or words
Beyond acceptance or approval
Beyond societal normality's
My truth is my beauty
My beauty is me

Who says that I am not beautiful?
Those who are ignorant as to the meaning of true beauty
Illiterate to the understanding of superiority
Those who possess the inability to appreciate distinguished quality
Unperceptive to persons of high caliber
Blind to an unbridled level of worth

I am value beyond all price
Entirely without flaws or defects
I am something excellent of my kind
Genuine, not counterfeit or imitation
I am of exceptional merit
A phenomenon by mere existence

I am my truth
My truth is my beauty
My beauty is me

Brooklynn White

$\mathcal{M}$y Beautiful Journey

Jenn Buchert
United States
Alopecia Unversalis

I thought I knew what love was at 16. I thought I knew what love was when I met my husband at 21. I thought I knew what love was when we wed at 24. I thought I knew what love was when I gave birth to our son at 29.

My husband and I were as happy as we could be. It was November of 2006. We just had our first child, our beautiful son Thomas. We built a beautiful home in Houston, Texas three years prior to having our son and had worked, saved, traveled and enjoyed our lives together. Everything was perfect. Life couldn't have been better.

I will NEVER forget that day I went to the dermatologist. It was life changing; my 7-month-old son was with me. Of course, he wanted to get out of his stroller and I had to work hard to keep him occupied as I waited in waiting room. At this point, I had already lost my eyebrows and eyelashes and only had about 30% of my hair left on my head. I was very self conscience, depressed and irritated that I had to go through this. I thought to myself "there are millions of women who have babies, why does my pregnancy hair loss have to be so severe!"

As I waited for my name to be called, people were staring at me and then looked at my son with pity in their eyes. I think most assumed I had cancer. I had to get used to feeling self-conscience. This was a new feeling for me. My entire life I was told how beautiful I was. I used to walk into a room and all heads would turn my way. I used to have thick, naturally blonde hair. The type of hair other girls hate you for. I was honored to be the Prom queen in high school and even won a beauty contest, Miss Junior Orange Bowl Queen. My sorority sisters would tell me I had Barbie hair. I did have Barbie hair. If I knew then what I know now, I would have appreciated how beautiful my hair was.

That day I learned I had an autoimmune disease.

Over the next weeks and months, I would vacillate from feeling deeply depressed and sad as if someone I loved died, to feeling angry, to being in denial.

I eventually decided to shave my head because I couldn't bear to see hair in the bathroom drain, on my pillow, on the floor, and on my son's clothes. My beautiful hair was everywhere as a constant reminder that it wasn't on my head anymore. I still remember as clear as day sitting in our guest bathtub while my husband shaved my head and our son watched as he sat in his baby excersaucer, playing with his toys, watching his daddy use this weird thing that makes a buzzing noise. Over the next few days and weeks I avoided mirrors. I couldn't even bring my son to a mirror to smile back at his own reflection because what I saw when I looked in the mirror was too painful for me to endure.

I would look forward to my son's naptime so I could cry really hard in private. I never wanted my son to see me upset. Although he was very young, he could still sense if his mommy was sad or upset. I would sing to him, "You are my sunshine, my only sunshine; you make me happy when skies are gray". I could never get to the end of the song because I would start crying midway through. My other "sunshine" was my husband. His presence was gentle and calm. I could always sense his strength and concern.

It has been almost 2 years now since I lost my hair. I have full blown Alopecia Universalis. There is not one single strand of hair on my entire body! From all of this, I have learned what true love is, I mean deep love, the kind that runs so deep, you know it's not leaving.

I have recently learned to embrace my hair loss and have most recently accepted it. I have come to realize it really isn't that important. How does that song go, "All you need is love"…

Some may look at me and feel sorry for me because maybe they think I have cancer or maybe they just feel sorry for me because I look so different. But I have it all. I have love. The love of myself, my husband, my son, my family and friends keeps me going.

I hope this story will inspire those who don't feel attractive, have lost their hair, or just have lost focus on what is important.

$\mathcal{I}$t takes Great Strength

Carol Jones
Canada
Alopecia Universalis

"To be different, takes great strength" I found myself telling my 13 year old daughter who is taking great pride in remaining unique from her peers. At her age I would have done anything to be "normal". I wasn't always AU, I developed alopecia areata by the tender age of one. It took many years of growing and learning of humility before I managed acceptance and gained self-esteem, which is why I was bewildered at my daughter's enthusiasm for wanting to be unique. I'm quite sure that the only difference here is that she has the option whereas, I didn't. Alopecia forced me to be rare, I didn't want to lose my hair - it just happened.

I don't remember getting alopecia because I was so young but that's not to say I don't understand the shock of losing your hair. What I do remember is that my adopted mother found a bald spot about the size of a silver dollar on the back of my head. She brought me to a doctor in Brampton, Ontario where we lived, who at first thought that I had just been laying on that part of my head too often until I developed a second spot.

At first it was silence and leering then around grade one it became whispering and giggling. It was also in grade one or two that I had to start defending myself against the older kids who would tease and taunt. By the time I, myself was in grade 4 I'd lost every friend and spent every recess (that I hadn't been in detention for) as the prime target for every aspiring bully.

To someone who was influenced heavily by the media and was always trying to keep up with the Jones' (pardon the pun), I was considered an embarrassment. My adopted mom just wanted to be like her sister with her own live dolly to dress up and I was her old, tattered Barbie doll. No matter how many pretty dresses she threw me into, she always led me to believe that I was this little bald, four-eyed, fat, freckled girl. My mother would only tell me to ignore the other kids, they weren't worth my effort anyhow but she couldn't understand what I endured. She didn't understand that the kids followed me when I walked away which of course invited the physical part of these conflicts. I was just a bad egg who ended up in the principal's office time and time again only to be blamed for everything that went on. The kids would blatantly lie, the teacher would blindly accept and that's how it went.

When I thought things couldn't get any worse. I was in grade 8 and my hair was falling out by the handfuls and was gone by winter. All the girls in my class were worried about their appearance for graduation pictures and junior prom as I was hauled out to the wig shop and fitted with a hairdo appropriate for a 45 year old woman. I looked stupid! It wasn't until I was almost an adult that children's wigs started becoming more readily available. Now, not only did my classmates threaten to take my new hair away but every gust of wind too.

As I got to college there wasn't as much teasing or pointing and giggling however, I did find myself becoming less embarrassed when someone asked about my hair. I was beginning to appreciate when someone could muster the guts to ask why

I'm bald.

I had gone to college for welding. This was a perfect job for me because I would never wear a wig while welding and preferred wearing a bandana at the time. I had a part time job through a temporary employment agency while I finished my course but it wasn't until I searched for a welding position outside of the agency that I began to realize I had a problem again. It wasn't so much the fact that I was bald but that I was a bald woman doing a man's job and this idea was just too perplexing therefore I never found a job (and I went to every place in town). I endured rude comments and questions and was treated as though I should be washing dishes or beat with an ugly stick. Any feeling of strength would fade as I looked for work. Because I have had such an assortment of jobs, I have learned that appearances can be detrimental to securing a position. Customer service, sales and many clerical positions don't normally employ bald or "non aesthetically pleasing" people to service their customers therefore it has been for those jobs that I have applied eye make-up and wigs and disguised my true identity. It's very hard doing this - having several looks. I find that when I wear a specific wig my personality changes slightly to suit my appearance.

I found the strength to face my fears and it started at home with my husband. I stopped wearing my wig around the house and he got used to it. I liked being free, not having to hide my condition from everyone. I liked that I didn't have to disguise myself every time I left my house. The power of being among a group of people with similar problems is astounding. Knowing you are not alone in your struggles and learning how others cope is essential for ones own personal gain.

I chose to be strong and now realize that you can't force someone to accept their situation before they are ready to face it. I now enjoy sharing my positive experiences with others and take pleasure in knowing I have eased their suffering by letting them know they are not alone. Although people comment on my alopecia and little kids stare at me like I'm from outer space, it doesn't bother me anymore.

I also refuse to admit that alopecia is a disease. I'm not unhealthy in any way and consider alopecia to be more of a condition if anything. I've found my sense of humor and always keep it at my side. I find it rewarding to educate others about alopecia. There are a few lessons I learned along the way that I didn't learn through school but the first and foremost is that I may have lost my hair but I haven't lost my smile. Staying positive is key because attitudes are contagious. I've gained my own acceptance through the positive attitudes of other people with alopecia and now wish to spread that same attitude.

The Show Must Go On

Catharina Wiberg
Sweden
Alopecia Universalis

When I discovered I had Alopecia started it felt like small animals were crawling inside my head. Then I got a small spot without hair. I went to the doctor and got injections of cortisone and a little hair came back. Then I started to loose the hair all over the head. I got more injection of cortisone but nothing helped. I could stand in the shower and I got the hair in my hand, it was such a terrible feeling. I was so unhappy and sad it helped to cry out my sadness that some of my personality just went away. What to do?

You feel helpless. The most terrible was when I lost my eyebrow and eyelashes. I really was depressed. I did not want to look in the mirror because I did not recognize myself.

Of course, I don't look like I did before but I have to make the best of the situation. I had to buy a wig which I did not like. I felt terrible, that it was someone else. When I saw photos of myself in the wig I did not recognize myself. Then it was a question if I should have real hair or synthetic.

Sometimes I use a scarf, especially in the summer. Most of all I would like to go outside with my bald head; but I do not like to see my head bald. When I see other women without hair I really understand why they are not using a wig. They must be very strong and have a good self confidence. One day I will also walk in town with my bald head but I am sure everyone would stare. Many are thinking that you have cancer when you are bald, but that is not true.

For a long time I would hide my head from my grandchildren but one day I decided that it is enough. So when we were sitting by the table I said that I can do magic. Can you believe that? One, two, three then I took off my wig and they really got a big surprise. That was about five years ago and now they want to borrow my wig.

"The show must go on"!

hrough Struggles Come Victory

Katrina Brewer
United States
Alopecia Areata

I yelled for my mother, and we thought "bad perm". It wasn't!

I went to a dermatologist who told me to braid my hair because there was nothing I could do and that it would all come out. Who wants to hear that as a teenager? I went into a really deep depression; I never came out of my room. I can remember the day I took the braids out and all my hair fell with it. It was the worst day of my life. I cried everyday and night.

With no hair came the wig. I thought it was cute as if I had much choice. People started the gossip she has on a wig and school became unbearable. I prayed so much at this time. I just wanted to be normal. I thought if I continued to pray that GOD would hear me and take it all away.

I never though that people I had known from middle school would even be a part of the pain. I still continued to pray and have faith, but I will say that I often questioned GOD and why would he burden me with this? I was raised to believe that he would not give me more then I could bear. At 15 that is the last thing you want to hear.

The depression got so bad I ended up at a psychiatrist who I despised because she did not have to go to school and hear people's comments and remarks. This was the time when my self image came into play and I felt like an outcast.

I contemplated taking my own life and have never told a soul until today. Right before I was to take the bottle of pills, I cried out to GOD to be saved and realized I could not hurt my family like that.

I continued to pray.

I made it through most of 10th 11th and 12th grade with about 95% of my hair. God allowed me to go to the prom with hair and that was the best gift that I could have received.

Life changed and I woke up one morning and decided I was done with treatment. The treatments were too much headache and at that point it was more about living my life. I have been blessed to have a strong support system and people who love me regardless. While I don't endure any day to day complications it is still apart of whom I am everyday of my life and will continue to be. It has been 10 years since I decided against treatments and it was the best thing for me and I have never looked back. Needless to say you will always be different. But is different always bad? I mean to think that you learn so much about people of all races and genders. This condition has allowed me to meet some really great people from all over the world. Do I still struggle with trust? Of course, but to think that as a human we all have something. For a small percentage of people with this condition it is obvious, and for others not so much.

Through all struggles come victory, and to be on the other side of it and know that I've won…To know in my heart that people, nor the disease have the last laugh, this has been the best part of me today. Do I still get sad? Yes, but on those days that I am, I realize that if I sit and dwell on it I might miss something important. I might miss my daughter's smile or something funny, and that is when I realize it could have been worse.

elf Reflection

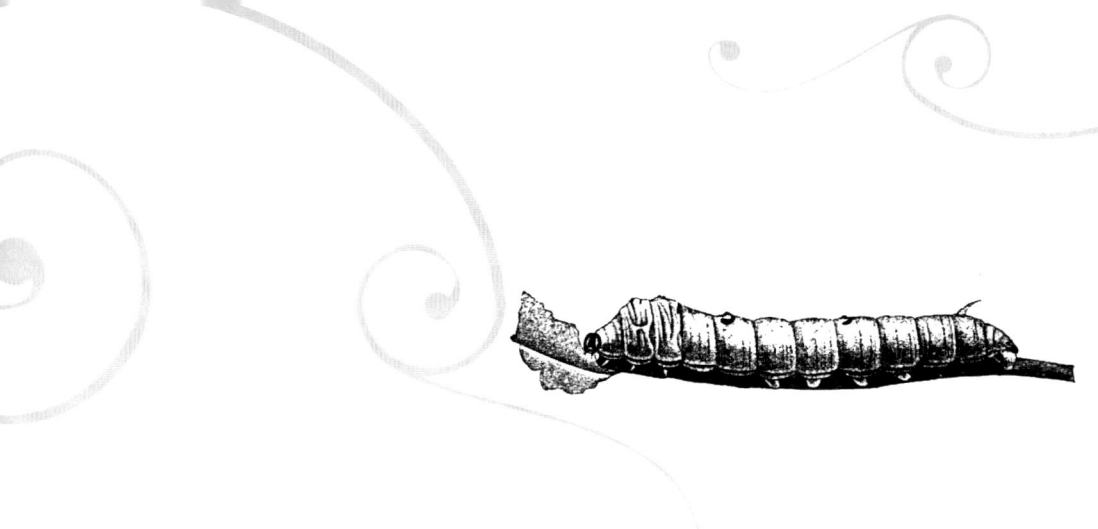

Growth

(Larva Stage)

"I had to come to the conclusion that one day I'll be gone from this earth. So as I viewed the ending, my present became clear and I can not change my past. Therefore embracing change is my only option."

Julia Crittendon

onfidence

For over 20 years she stood quietly,
Frozen in time…
Listening to lies…
For she was groovin' to the vibe of society's melodic rhythms
Its definition of beautiful,
And it's sounding portrait of who she should strive to be,
But, this reality created a statuette of low self-esteem and inferiority,

"All about them; so little about me…" became her conscience.
"Happiness?
It's totally unreachable…
For how can I achieve such a dream
When I don't…
When I can't…
When magazine cutouts plaster the walls, and mirrors are everywhere…
The images…
I try so hard,
My hair, my weight, my skin…
I try so hard,
I can't measure up…
But still,
I try so hard!"

Yet, the truth was beautiful in the most perfect ways,
The woman standing was talented beyond measure…
Sista could sing,
She could write,
She was "mean" in a kitchen,
And she knew how to eloquently embrace the lives of so many,

A lover of people…
A spirit nurturer…
She even possessed the best kind of beauty;
That which was natural!
Yet, the only thing she ever allowed her eyes to see
Or, her ears to hear… was how she possessed difference.

For in her mind,
Difference followed connotations of negativity
The tragedy of her sight was being blinded from the truth of her uniqueness,

cont.

And, oneself being divinely fashioned by God,

Therefore, stress invited the brink of a meltdown,
But, inadvertently a blessing was carried,
An overload of emotions rained through...
And finally,
Something occurred to set thoughts free,

An epiphany was rendered
It was evident...
No change to her mindset would be her death.

In hindsight,
Faith glared into her eyes
She held onto Him tightly...
"Who am I?"
Finding her identity became her mission...
And she dug deeply into the crevice of everything that loved really hard.

Ironically, "everything" also included her heart...
And in it...
She found beauty,
She found acceptance,
She found courage,
And she found the ability to spread her wings.

As she began to soar into the possibilities of life,
She did what she had never imagined...
She found happiness,
And, she began to live.
That was the most profound melody of her existence...
For she was now groovin' to a vibe called...
Confidence!

DeAndria "Tennessee" Slayton

A Magnificent View

Shannon Cox
United States
Alopecia Areata

"I'm not so sure about this," my voice quivered and my hands shook as I tried to put on my lip-liner.

"Then why are you going?" my husband asked.

"Because I want to," I said.

"Then why are you crying?" he asked.

I shrugged and looked up towards the ceiling in hopes of stopping the tears from spilling out and messing up my fresh makeup. I took a few deep breaths looked in the mirror, straightened up and gave myself, and my husband a nervous smile. I kissed my three small children, put on my coat and hat for the chilly November afternoon, and climbed into the car alone.

I felt okay for a few minutes, but suddenly the 35 mile trip felt very long. I felt a nervous flutter in my stomach again and picked up my cell phone. I set it back down and took a few more deep breaths. I listened to the radio then picked up the phone again and pushed the number for my sister-in-law, and she answered.

"Hello, Allison?" I began and we shared the normal pleasantries.

"Are you okay, Shan?"

"Yes, I, well, I am just on my way to that lunch," I stammered.

"You are right now?" Her voice raised in excitement. "That is so cool! You are going to have such a great time!"

"Well…," I paused and blinked, willing the tears again not to mess up my make-up. "I'm kind of starting to freak out a bit. I'm not sure if I want to go."

Allison immediately gave me the reassurances that I needed and reminded me of all the reasons that I was looking forward to this lunch. If only I had somebody with me, just one person that I knew. But having a familiar voice reassuring me was helpful.

"And think of what good you might be doing to change stigmas," she said. "Do you know that not too long ago pregnant women couldn't do a lot of things because it was inappropriate for them to be seen in certain settings?"

Suddenly I recalled an experience that my own mother had been through. She became pregnant during her last semester of college, just before she was to do her student teaching and receive her teaching certificate in education. She was married and responsible, but when the staff learned of her pregnancy she was not allowed to do her student teaching. They seemed to think her appearance would create an unprofessional and inappropriate image for the classroom. Luckily in the 50 years since that time, there have been those (like my mom) who refused to let an appearance stop them and things have changed. A few years ago I was able to teach a university class up until I was nine months pregnant. The thought of being a part of changing the way society views beauty gave me a clearer sense of purpose and helped me feel better about continuing down to the lunch.

I felt less alone and thanked Allison as I pulled into the parking garage. Once I found a spot, I turned off the engine and sat quietly for a few minutes. I was late. Would I be the last to arrive? What if nobody was there? And why did the lunch have to be in a very large restaurant in the middle of a large downtown mall? I took off my hat and looked in the mirror. My stomach was turning somersaults. I clasped my hands together and said a short prayer. Then it came to me. Not a voice, just a thought a very clear thought. "It's time to make your choice."

It took only a minute to decide.

"I choose to be beautiful," I said to my reflection and got out of the car. I straightened my dress and straightened my spine. I rolled my shoulders back and lifted the crown of my head towards the sky. I put on a layer of lip gloss. I smiled and began to walk. It was a long walk and it was cold. I noticed people looking at me. I glanced at them only long enough to smile and kept going.

Entering the restaurant I was relieved to spot my table immediately. The founder of the organization that had arranged the lunch stood and welcomed me. I recognized her from the photos on her website. Her smile was warm and inviting. Although she was nearly a foot shorter than I in my tall boots, her hug was huge. I sat down and immediately felt more at ease. All of the women smiled at me. There was an instant connection. We all shared so much and could relate on so many levels. Our eyes spoke volumes before introductions were made.

We spent several hours talking about everything you can imagine—especially our experiences with the disease that brought us all together. I have an auto-immune disease called Alopecia Areata. It started at the age of 12 with just one bare spot the size of a quarter on the back of my scalp. The spots came and went over the next nine years, and then I experienced a period of about 18 months with total hair loss. It had grown back and was pretty stable for the next eight years. Then, two years ago, I went through a rugged bout with Hepatitis A, and lost all of my hair in just a two week period. I also lost my eyebrows and many of my lashes as well as patches of hair on the rest of my body. This lunch was the first time that I had gone out in public without a wig or even a scarf on my head. I had made the choice to be beautiful and I felt it.

Driving home, I felt as if a huge burden had been lifted from my shoulders. I felt that everything was going to be okay.

Six months have gone by and I now realize that day was definitely the catalyst for change that I needed. From that point on my whole concept of beauty began to evolve. I no longer have to try to convince myself that I am beautiful. I know that I am. And it has nothing to do with my appearance.

It is difficult, I believe, for all of us to deal with the image of beauty. Most of us do not fit into the mold that has been shown to us. The images that the media is constantly stressing, urge us to believe that there are only certain ways to be beautiful and that we never really measure up. We are lead to believe that we are only beautiful when our outward appearance fits very strict guidelines. Yet strangely, often those who are so revered for their physical beauty are very insecure and do not feel beautiful inside. So, somehow, the concept of the outward physical beauty that we see on TV and in magazines is flawed. I now define beauty differently for myself.

There is beauty in my calling as a mother. When I see my children thriving, when

I see them perform an act of kindness, when they laugh in pure joy, I recognize my beauty. There is beauty in my passion for serving the children in Haiti (my son's native country). When I accomplish something and see a seed of change planted within a poverty-stricken family, I recognize my beauty. There is beauty in my spirituality and my faith. When I believe that the real me is not my appear-

ance, but a being who was created in the image of divinity and who will live on in the eternities after this mortal body has turned to dust, I recognize my beauty.

It has not been easy reaching the place where I am today. I often felt like an insurmountable ascent. I also recognize that I still have a long way to go. But having climbed so far up the mountain, I find the world quite breathtaking. I want to climb higher and faster. Also, I want all those who read these words to come up here too, and share in this magnificent view.

inding the Path

Yolonda Johnson
United States
Alopecia Universalis

I have always felt in my heart that I was not beautiful. Through-out my life I would always get compliments on how pretty I was, and of course friends and family would tell me, but for some reason I have never felt beautiful. I figured that if I keep my appearance up and I lose some weight I would be a beautiful female, but still no matter what I never felt beautiful.

I think about when I went through a very stressful moment with the first man that I would ever consider spending the rest of my life with, was when I noticed some major hair loss. This time it seemed as if I had gone to sleep one night and when I had awaken the next day about 30 percent of my hair was gone. My hair loss happened so swiftly that I was devastatingly shocked.

My journey begins…

I could not believe this was happening to me. I have always taken very good care of my hair. My hair is what many would call healthy or "good hair". In a matter of maybe 6 months I had become a self-made expert on manipulating fake hair with hair glue to create amazing hair-do's on my head, and not realizing that this was only making matters worse. I did not feel confident wearing the fake hair I guess the thought of a track showing or falling out while I was in public had a lot to do with that. One day I did my hair beautifully and I went to work. I noticed a tract of curls had fallen out of my head onto my shoulder. Being in complete shock I reached my hand into my head, and that was when I realized that all of the tracts of weave were just falling out of my head in public at work and there were people all around me…The nightmare had come true I still could not believe that had happened… Even after being completely embarrassed from my tracts falling from my head I allowed my insecurities and society to pressure me into feeling I had to continue using weave rather then walking around without hair and that is exactly what I did. Hindsight is amazing had I known the total effects that weave would have on my hair loss I would have been more mindful of my choices in dealing with my hair loss.

So I began wearing wigs. I started wearing the wigs in the winter months and I thought to myself that I should have done this sooner. I thought that I should have worn the wigs sooner at least until it got hot outside then I felt like I was being cooked through my skull with the wigs on my head. It was funny because I ran into an old friend one summer and we sat down to talk for a minute and he asked me if I was hot. I thought to myself what the heck do you think but instead I replied no. I guess the ocean of sweat coming from up under the wig was a good indication that I was hot, very hot with my wig on.

I found that small path that led to me when one day my good friend and play-sister, who dared my boldness and suggested that I go hairless outside my home. This was truly unimaginable to me, just plain crazy talk. So of course I did it, I left the house with no hair, no weave, no hot fuzzy hat, no scarf, nothing on my head.

It was kind-of funny when I left the house that day we went to my friend's job. I walked twenty feet and suddenly busted into tears. I tried to hide it but I couldn't. My friend turned around and asked me what was wrong. I told her that this wasn't as easy as I thought it would be. I finally gained my composure and proceeded on to my destination. From then on it just got better and better.

Through prayer, friends, and loved ones I am now at the point where I can walk out side of my front door with confidence.

I HAVE FINALLY FOUND MY--- BEAUTIFUL --- SELF!

Reflection

Daria Rowe
United States
Alopecia Universalis

It was a beautiful chestnut brown, straight and silky. I usually wore it long and, as I got older, I would often put golden highlights in it to give it even more sparkle and shine.

I was a sophomore in college, I was studying for my final exams with some friends. For whatever reason, I noticed what felt like a bald spot on the nape of my neck. Curious, I flipped my head over and asked them about it. My best friend started laughing and said, "Oh my God....you're not going to believe this, but you have a bald spot!" And I did.

I remember the horror of watching it pile up in the shower drain and on the bathroom floor; constantly having to clean the hair out my hairbrush; or just getting clumps tangled in my fingers if I would happen to run my fingers through my hair. Graphic and disheartening reminders of what was happening to me.

Luckily for me, I had my boyfriend (now my husband) Keith. Keith was, and always has been, my best friend and biggest supporter. That's not to say he's been easy on me. In fact, he's always been pretty tough in discouraging any pity parties. But he's always been there treating me exactly the same way as the day he met me, never seeming to love me any less or think me any less beautiful.

After college, Keith and I married. My hair hung more than halfway down my back. One year later, it was gone completely, absolutely gone. To say I was devastated would be an understatement. Losing my hair robbed me of any and all self confidence and pride. It also confused the hell out of me. Why would this happen? I'd been told all along the bald spots were due to stress. Well, now I was a newlywed. I was done with school. I was happy! It just didn't make sense.

Where did it leave me? Twenty-five years old, bald and unbelievably depressed. I was feeling ugly, sad, exhausted, and ashamed. Wanting to go out dancing with my friends but scared to do so because I didn't want my wig to slip off.

The doctors couldn't tell me why my hair was falling out, but they did tell me that taking oral steroids might bring it back. I began taking heavy doses of prednisone. Miraculously, the hair began to grow back. I was ecstatic. I was going to be normal again! Of course, I gained a bunch of weight and my face swelled like a pumpkin, but I was happy anyway. Within a year and a half, my hair was long enough that I could go wigless.

I would continue to lose patches of hair here and there for the next 10 years even though I continued taking the prednisone. During that time, I would also develop three other autoimmune disorders - thyroid disease (Hashimoto's), eczema and rheumatoid arthritis. But more importantly, I would also give birth to three beautiful daughters and begin my own successful home childcare business.

At the age of 35, I lost all my hair once again. But this time, it's different. Medically speaking, it's worse, as this time around I've also lost my eyebrows, eyelashes and body hair. But it also just feels different. Maybe it's maturity; maybe it's the fact that I'm surrounded by so much love; maybe it's that I've been through this before. I don't know and I don't care. What I do know is that this time around, I'm not going to sit home and feel ashamed. I'm going dancing and I'll laugh if my wig slips a bit. I'm going to the pool wearing nothing on my head but a baseball cap to block the sun's rays. I won't wear a wig at all around my house or neighborhood or when I'm with my friends. I will teach my children acceptance and show them that people can be beautiful in many different ways.

I look at it like this. I haven't changed just because my hair has. I'm still the same smart, caring, friendly, silly person I've always been. That's not to say that I don't wish I still had my hair. Let's be realistic….of course, I do! But I sure don't miss taking an hour to get ready in the morning. I sure don't miss shaving my legs every day in the summertime! Being bald has its ups and downs, just like every other aspect of life. I've finally come to realize that my friends and family will love me no matter what my hair looks like and, if I'm still beautiful to them, that's all that really matters. I try to focus on the upside and leave it at that. And if I ever do feel like throwing myself a pity party, then I know my husband will surely step in and break it up!

*W*ind Be Still
Mandy Grimm
United States
Alopecia Areata

I've never known anything else. For a long time I don't think I realized I was that different until I hit junior high and high school. As a teenager I just wanted to blend in with everyone else. It was hard to relate to the other girls when they started shaving legs, plucking eyebrows, and deciding on how their hair would be worn to the formal and semi formal dances. I very rarely let someone else touch my hair because it gave me such anxiety to think about how they would react if they saw a bald spot. I usually tried to style my hair myself in the best way I could or sometimes I'd have help from a friend or my mom. I did play a couple sports and it was really hard when the girls would want to braid their hair and look the same. I couldn't do that. I was able to wear my hair in a low ponytail and that was it, braiding would only expose what I worked hard to keep to myself.

Going to college and meeting new people made me really nervous. I think a lot of it was to have to experience something outside my comfort zone.

Once equipped with the new knowledge of myself and my degree in my hand I set out to take on the working life.

Blending in is still something I try to do and I don't ache to be the center of attention My hair must lay a certain way to hide the bald patches trying to make their debut and the wind is my worst enemy. Applying make up used to consist of eye shadow, liner and mascara but with the recent loss of part of my eyelashes that has been whittled down to shadow and liner. I don't draw in eyebrows since my hair is blond and skin is fair thus, people rarely notice. My hair is fine and naturally thin already so applying some foaming mousse and good blow dry gives it some body. My daily achievement is to feel good about myself and it helps to have friends, family and my boyfriend to give me constant reminders that I am beautiful.

y Worth

Lousie MacNeil Howell
Canada
Alopecia Universalis

In the summer of 1987, I was 11 years old. My brother, sister and I were at the community swimming pool, splashing around, when my sister called out across the water "Louise! What happened to your head?"

I had no idea what she was talking about - until she swam over to me and explained that there was a big bald spot on the top of my head.

Fast forward

In the summer of 2002, I was about to begin my fourth year as a teacher. I was in a new city, at a new school. I had just moved into my first apartment the year before, and my alopecia seemed to have gone into remission. I hadn't reduced any stress - in fact probably added more, with my career, but I had started using a product that I purchased from the Shopping Channel (I know I know, but I was desperate). I don't know if using this product had a placebo effect, or if my body was just giving it a rest on the alopecia front, but about

90% of the hair that was missing, started growing back. I was finally beginning to be able to wear my hair how I liked. I was ecstatic! The product was expensive, though, and eventually I ran out. Again, I didn't think much about it - my hair was growing, and that was what mattered.

In October of 2002, I was at my parents' house visiting for (Canadian) Thanksgiving. I was in the shower, washing my hair, and when I pulled my hands away from my head... 95% of the hair that had been on my head, had come out in my hands. No pain, no forewarning, just *ping* hair in my hands.

I panicked, and started screaming. My mother came in and also panicked. When we eventually calmed down, I was in shock. I sat there with my hair in my hands, staring. What was I going to do? How was I going to explain this to people? How could I go out in public like this? More importantly... who would ever love me, looking this way? I had just recently started getting to know a really great guy, and I was sure that he would run for the hills the second I told him about this bizarre thing that had happened to me.

Over the next few weeks, the rest of the hair on my head fell out. Eventually I lost my eyelashes, then my eyebrows, and then the rest of the hair on my body. My doctor increased the steroid dosage, increased the steroid injections, and I learned to draw on my eyebrows.

Here is what these medical interventions did for me: In the first year I gained about 100lbs because of the extreme hunger the medication caused. The shots left me with two or three hairs growing at the area where the shots were, but they would fall out, too. My self esteem and self-worth plummeted. Not only was I bald, which at the time I equated with unattractive, but I had also put on so much weight that I wasn't comfortable in my own skin, and none of my clothes fit me properly. I would avoid looking in the mirror as much as possible. I felt like an alien.

After a couple of years, I decided that since these treatments weren't working for me, and were in fact causing more problems than I thought they were worth, I would just stop.

At first I would do anything to cover up the fact that I had alopecia. I slept with my wig on. I wore false eyelashes. Now I am much more open about it. I wear my wig to work, because I don't want my students concentrating on my bald head (and also because my head gets cold!), but they all know that it's a wig and that I have alopecia. If they have questions, I answer. At home, my wig lives on the table by the front door; as soon as I walk in the door, the wig comes off. I often don't go out without my wig on. I am a shy, private person, so I don't enjoy the stares that I get, and the whispers that I hear - I would rather someone speak to me directly, ask me a question, instead of making assumptions. On the rare occasion that someone does come up and ask, I explain that I'm perfectly healthy, aside from the autoimmune disorder that made me lose my hair. Will my hair grow back? I don't know. If it does, I'm okay with it and if it doesn't... I'm okay with it. People usually seem surprised at that.

You may be wondering about the great guy, Rob, who I had been dating when my hair first fell out.   That conversation (which, because I am a chicken, happened on the phone), went something like this:

"Rob, I have to tell you something. I would really love to keep you as a friend, after this, if you're comfortable with it".

"Are you breaking up with me?"

"No, no. But I need to tell you. I have an autoimmune disorder. I lost pretty much all my hair today because of it. It's not contagious, and it's not any kind of deadly thing - it's just the hair. So anyway... can we still be friends?"

"Why are you assuming that I'm breaking up with you because of this? I love you. You're beautiful.   You were beautiful with hair, you're beautiful now. I can't wait to see you."

We were married on August 19, 2006.

It took awhile, but I realize that just because I don't have hair, doesn't mean I'm not beautiful. I'm finally - after nearly 15 years of trying to hide my alopecia-comfortable with who I am - and who I am is a wife, a daughter, a sister, a friend, a teacher, a learner... and I just happen to have alopecia, just like I happen to have blue eyes. It is part of me, but it's not all of me. I'm a pretty great person, and my hair (or lack thereof) has absolutely nothing to do with my worth as a human being.

Self Reflection

_____

_____

_____

_____

_____

_____

_____

_____

_____

_____

_____

_____

_____

_____

_____

_____

_____

_____

_____

_____

_____

_____

_____

_____

The Transition

(Pupa Stage)

"Transformation

Emerging

…what a miracle"

Julia Crittendon

ransitions

Like a butterfly,
I am beautiful
from the top
of my head
to the bottom
of my feet.

Like a butterfly
I have come
into my own
I have been
wrapped tight;
encased in silk,
Lying dormant,
Growing, learning,
Praying and understanding
Who I am
and patiently awaiting
my moment
to emerge,
whole.

Like a butterfly
I have arrived
I spread my wings
for all to see
and to share
in my message,
that I am beautiful
from the top
of my head
to the bottom
of my feet,
And I
am One
to be reckoned
with!

Forever Amber

 Why Not Me?

Holly Oyler
United States
Alopecia Universalis

When I was three or four years old I remember playing store in the house and using items from the kitchen. At age seven, I decided to open a lemonade stand on the side of the two-lane country road we lived on. For day's, I sat there and talked to Monopoly, my imaginary friend that lived in our mail box. Lots of cars went by, but no one would stop. Friday was grocery day and Mother strongly suggested I close up shop and go with her. While we were there, I noticed that the busy part of the small store was the strawberry section in the produce isle. At home we had a huge garden, full of strawberries; I took my 50 cent weekly allowance and talked the store owner into selling me those cute little strawberry baskets for a penny each.

The next morning I was up early and in the garden, filling my baskets. I put them on my table with a sign that said "50 cents each". Cars started stopping and at one point, Mother had to come out of the house and help me. Within hours, all fifty baskets were gone and I had a grand total of $25.00. I called my Dad and asked him to stop at the grocery store on the way home and buy more baskets and some brown paper bags. He did, not having a clue what I was doing. When he found out I was selling his strawberry patch, he was less than amused, but he let me continue.

The next day I filled the baskets again and set them out on my table. Only this time, when a person bought the berries, I gently put them in the paper bags and kept the baskets to refill. At seven years old, I found the beauty of niche' marketing. Drivers on a country road did not need lemonade, but they did need strawberries for dinner. Little did I know where that one experience would lead me in life.

Alopecia Areata came and went throughout my childhood without much attention paid to it by me. I loved fashion, so I started wearing hats and scarves. My world consisted of perfect people in perfect makeup and clothes. Not much else earned my attention, except Ray the man I married in 1973. In the spring of 1975 we were transferred from Kentucky to Los Angeles because of Ray's job. Once there, my Father became ill and I was commuting back and forth once a week for three months until his death. When I returned to LA my world started tumbling out of control. My hair started falling out again, my sense of self was gone and I retreated to our bedroom and would not come out. Within months, my hair was completely gone. No one could tell me how to help myself and the industry I had worked so long and hard in totally abandoned me. I scheduled an appointment with a huge national company only to arrive and be told "sorry, we only work on normal people". I was crushed.

So, I now, at 62, I ask myself "why not me" when it comes to my hair loss. What better person to help others deal with their image needs? Knowing the lives I have touched so personally gets me through the really bad and down times I experience and yes, they still come around every so often.

When I ventured into the chemotherapy market one of my first clients died after six months. When her Mother went into check on her, she found her with a note in hand saying "thank Holly for letting me die with dignity". I knew the moment her Mother handed me that note that I was in the right place, at the right time in my life and that it had all been pre arranged by a higher being.

Now, after so many years I also understand why none of my dolls ever had hair. I always chose the bald ones and if I did receive one with hair, I would cut it down to the scalp and off within a day or so.

Amazing how childhood things become so clear and full circle in our lives.

ust Live

Charmaine Findley
United States
Cicatricial Alopecia

My head felt like it was exploding!

I immediately went to wearing wigs; which at 19 years of age, was more traumatic than having Alopecia. It was easy for me to tell everyone that I had this auto immune deficiency, because with so much focus on glamour and hair, especially in the black community, it was a lot easier for me to tell the truth than to have everyone whisper about my wigs behind my back. But still, wigs at 19, after having years of "normal" (if there is such a thing) hair, was traumatic. I was criticized by the people who passed judgment. But one day I grew up…just like that…I realized that this was not traumatic, it was who I am. It was me; and I was…AM…beautiful. My hair did not define my beauty, the person I was within defined my beauty.

So today, I am open with my alopecia. To family, boyfriends, girlfriends, co-workers…they all know. They accept me for who I am and could care less about the wig on my head. Many of them ask why I wear a wig. "Just go bald…be free" they say. But that is one thing I still cannot do. The sores that I endured at the onset of Alopecia caused scarring on my scalp and sometimes they (the sores) still appear. So to diffuse the attention, I just find a wig that looks natural and fits me.

I actually enjoy wig shopping…I've had long hair, short hair, black hair, blonde hair…and if I have a bad hair day or am feeling spontaneous, I just stop by the wig store!

Alopecia has never defeated me because as I put things into perspective, I realize that I could have been fighting lupus or cancer, or could have lost a limb. But instead, I lost a little…okay a lot…of hair. Oh well, that's who I am. Being beautiful just the way I am….and embracing it! So my motto, Live well, Live happy…no matter what, Just Live! It's just that easy…with or without hair.

Charmaine Findley

 Standing Still

Tamara Cramer Bornemann
Netherlands
Alopecia Universalis

We all want to believe and have faith. I am gaining more faith in myself everyday and thank God and the divined angels daily.

Yes it was tough, especially my years as a teenager, like every teenager I wanted to be normal and perfect and my alopecia wasn't working with me. At the age of 19 I went to live on my own, chose my own study and I was in bloom. I did some modelling work, went out every night and felt beautiful, grown up with plenty of boyfriends. Finally there was Tam.

I will never forget those times. I ended up with a special boyfriend and lived for 8 years with him and got married. In 2004 we divorced and I was single again. I was ok with it because the divorce was my own choice and my ex husband and I were still very good friends.

One Friday night I was watching a film and I started to cry because it was such a sad film. But then I couldn't stop crying and lost total control of myself. After hours of non stop crying I found out that I so missed my hair. Until that day I never said I missed my hair and I was always the strong bald girl. I faced my pain and sadness what I have been hiding since the day I got Alopecia.

I call Alopecia an emotional rollercoaster, but I am learning to enjoy that roller-coaster more and more each day and take the twists and turns as for what they are. Sometimes I need a little help from people to talk about it and I am getting better at that.

In 2007 I asked for help from a mental and spiritual coach and he helped me to face the grieving of my hair loss. I never had grieved over my hair loss when I was a little girl and the grieving was trying to get out. This was very hard for me to do. But after licking my heart wounds I started to feel better and stronger.

This world is already a hectic world where often we forget to stand still and look around to the people next to us. I want to stand still and say: "what a beautiful day, what a beautiful world" and interact with the people on this planet.

Alopecia can be a great opportunity to raise awareness for a beautiful world where people learn not to judge others by rules how our society tells us to look like or act like. Rules like what is normal and what is not normal. We are not robots, we are people of the world, we have feelings and compassion.

Beauty comes out from our hearts and it's the glow that is around us everyday. A smile can make a big difference; it's a sign of the beauty that is in our heart and soul. A smile doesn't cost energy it will only give us the energy we all so want. We all want to love and be loved. Loving oneself can help with that, smile when you look in the mirror. Yes we aren't perfect, we aren't who we wanted to be when we were children and made innocent wishes.

But we are learning to love ourselves everyday with support and awareness. We can succeed our inner wish of acceptance towards ourselves and from others. Every person in the world is worth the air we breathe and the love what is surrounding us. Give your self the permission to love and be loved. We all are beautiful, show your smile, and show your heart!

rossroads

Yvonne King
United States
Alopecia Totalis

My first encounter with Alopecia Areata was in 1993, at that time I was dying my hair and perming my hair like crazy. I got a brilliant idea to try a hair care product that I saw on a late night infomercial. It was suppose to be all natural to relax curly hair. Yeah well, silly me bought into that "infomercial" and purchased a kit. I put this "all natural stuff from Brazil" in my hair and guess what happened.

I have been living with Alopecia Areta off and on for 15 years. Now for the past

two years it has progressed to Alopecia Totalis. I am completely bald, I have no patches, and there is no sign of hair returning, at least enough to call it hair. It's been over 18 months since I shaved hair from my head other than the occasional gray strands. There is one side of my head where the baby hair wants to come in on the hairline, but that's it.

About a year ago I started going into the world showing my baldness on the weekends when going out to the store or just out with my husband. I would wear my wigs to work and for dressy events.

Recently I revealed my head at work, wearing no head coverings at all. It's been 6 or 7 months now and it was hard at first but I was able to get through it. Because I had to build my self up and teach my workplace about Alopecia Awareness, before I reveled myself the shock wasn't that bad. I also had to make a point of not wearing wigs to work to show that I was not hiding and that I was proud of my pretty shaped dome... I felt I had to prove this to myself and the others around me.

Now, that I have placed myself out there...I want to wear my wigs again from time to time... But I'm having mixed feelings like, if I were to wear my wigs again... I would have to deal with querying looks... the questions and comments when people feel they just have to say something to me. Or for the most part, I don't want to feel like I'm giving up the fight of acceptance...I don't want to give off that message at all.

But, isn't this my free choice? Something I originally wanted to be the message in my Alopecia Awareness? This is my quandary.

There are days when I feel really strong about my beautiful bald head and other days when the air conditioning is just too cold, and I wish I had my wig... Along with the fact that I'm seeing a lot of cute styles and colors in wigs.

There are some who thinks going out in public is inappropriate and can be viewed as a fade. I don't think there is an inappropriate place for baldness, unless you allow someone to tell you so. But I have also always been one to go the other way, especially when I am being told I shouldn't.

This ironically always puts me in a crossroad... Should I mix it up with a wig one day and confuse the mess out of people the next day with my baldness... I like doing things like that, so I think from now on...
I will MIX IT UP!

Taking the First Step

Char Hartman
United States
Alopecia Universalis

She freaked out at first, calling the doctors and even taking me to the emergency room. She didn't know what was wrong and was more worried than I was. I thought it's just a bite that left a scar, what's the big deal.

Well, the tests came back fine and I was sent to see a dermatologist. At that time he diagnosed me with Alopecia Areata.

When I was in the 8th grade I decided it was time to educate my classmates about Alopecia. I decided that my Science Project would be about Alopecia. I researched the topic and talked to them about it. My classmates were actually wonderful; I wasn't teased except for maybe one time. They knew I had it, and seemed to forget.

In 2001, I was almost in a fatal car crash. I lost my grandfather and a very good friend in a matter of a couple of months. The doctors thought I would lose all my hair due to stress, but I didn't. A year later, my parents lost their house to a tornado. Even I thought this is it; this is going to make me bald. It didn't. Instead, my father started to get bald spots. He was diagnosed with alopecia areata at the age of 45. I was 19 and had been dealing with Alopecia since I was 11.

In 2004 I married a wonderful supportive man. He knew that there was always a chance I might go bald, but he accepted me for me. I never thought I would go bald, until 2005, when my hair stopped growing back. I became scared and thought maybe I should stop being stubborn and see a doctor again. I decided with my doctor and family that I should just accept the inevitable, and deal with the situation. It was time! I went with my mom and husband to go wig shopping.

It was strange putting a wig on my head. Once I did I realized just how much of my hair was actually missing. I looked so different. It was a different feeling to have fake hair on my head. My husband, my family, and co-workers were very supportive.

I wore bandannas to work almost everyday, and almost everyday I was asked by someone, "Are you sick?"

It can be hard because you feel at times that you are losing your femininity. It takes time to cross that bridge to knowing that it doesn't matter that you don't have hair, you are still you. I go out in public with my bandanna on and hold my head high. I walk around my house and yard and even once in awhile at work, completely bald. I'm still me, just minus all of my hair.

My motto is "Life happens", and I just think of this whenever I start to feel like things are getting out of control. I have to realize some things I can't control, and I just have to adjust and move on. God made me this way for a reason and I have learned to accept it. There are still days when I wish I had hair, but wishing will get me nowhere. Once we accept ourselves for who we are, then others will do the same. We just have to be the ones to take that first step.

Self Reflection

Unfolding

(Butterfly Stage)

I am not my hair
I am not this skin
I am not your expectations no
I am not my hair
I am not this skin
I am a soul that lives within

India Aria

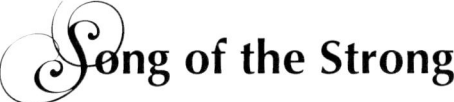Song of the Strong

You stand tall
Shoulders back, chest out
You stand proud
Inspiration
Glowing in your frame
Shimmering aura
You roam the plains
You own the plains
The once shadowed soul
The now butterfly floats
Ferocious
Strong
Lioness on her own
Defeatless
It is YOU they cheer, for you can do all
Conqueror of fear
Clear minded
Appearance unblinded
Kind woman unsilenced
Sing your song...
We are listening

D.R. Hill

New Reality

Yokasta Martinez
United States
Alopecia Areata

I first remember hearing about my father's family in California when I was 4 years old. I remember listening to my parents argue about my father going to visit them. I also remember my father coming home from that trip with a baby. The baby turned out to be my sister, and my parents' arguing had been about whether or not to retrieve her from my aunt – my father's sister who is in fact her birth mother – who was a teenager at the time and totally incapable of raising a child. It was also during this time that I started second grade. In case you're wondering how a 4-year-old manages to start school in the 2nd grade, I was a very gifted and precocious child. I started reading at age 3 and could comprehend what I read at a 6th grade level, as well as do math at a 4th grade level. Kindergarten simply could not keep up with my academic needs; however, because of my age I was allowed to return to the kindergarten classroom every day during recess for naptime. I was very excited to get up and put on my uniform every day for school and have my mother fix my hair into two perfect pigtails – I thought it made me look very grown up. As always, my head always hurt for hours afterward, but to be honest, I never paid much attention to that.

My first clue that something was wrong came one winter morning as I was getting ready for school. We were following our established routine, and I was having my pigtails fixed when suddenly my mother stopped what she was doing and took me into the bathroom and looked at my head under a brighter light. After a moment she told me not to move and then went into my bedroom and proceeded to take the pillowcases off the pillows and remove the sheets and blankets from my bed, turn them inside out, and shake them thoroughly. She then ran out of the room and checked the bathroom and kitchen drawers. I watched all this with a growing sense of confusion and a growing feeling that something was not right. Finally, my mother came into the room where she left me with my grandmother and asked me if I had been pulling on my hair at all. I told her that I hadn't. She then asked me if I had been playing with any scissors or knives at all. Because I knew those items were not toys and I was not allowed to play with them, I answered no. (That and I really hadn't been playing with them.) Finally, she asked me if I had been allowing my classmates to play in my hair. I told her that I hadn't.

While she was asking me these questions, my grandmother was looking at my head and examining my scalp to see if there were any cuts or bruises to explain.

My grandmother, who was a former nurse and a very practical person, got a seamstress' tape measure and measured the size of the two spots in my head. They measured the size of a dime and the size of a quarter. The smaller of the two spots was located in the top of my head, near my hairline, and the larger of the two was in the back of my head, close to the nape of my neck. Because my hair was very long and thick at the time, the spots were easily covered up. My grandmother advised my mother to just watch my hair for a couple of weeks to see if the spots would grow back in by themselves.

They never did. In fact, they got worse.

By this time, I was 5 years old and completely bald.

I think it is a remarkable ability for a small child to only focus on the here and now, rather than the long-term effects a major life change will have. Initially, when the first spots started appearing in my head, I just accepted it as something happened and that Mommy and Daddy and Honey would take care of it and that was that. It didn't exist any more.

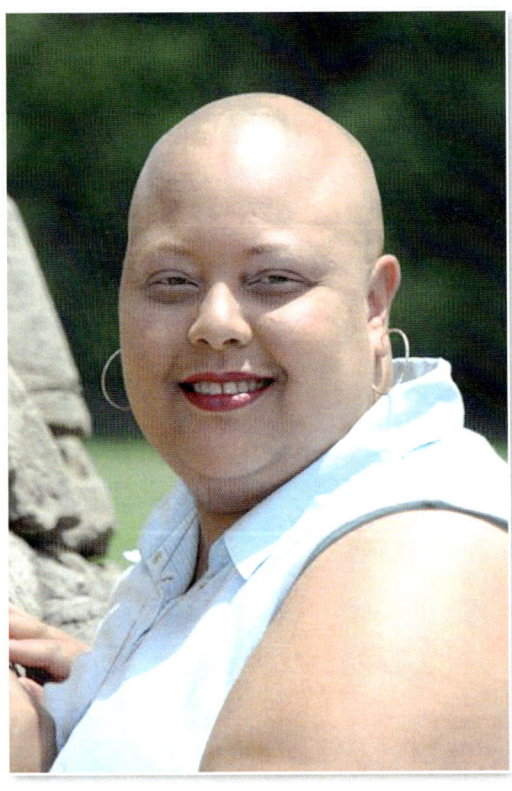

Oh, how I wish things could have remained that way. Unfortunately, one of life's harshest lessons is that things never turn out the way that we always like, regardless of the circumstances.

My mother, always overprotective in the best of circumstances, and my grandmother, to whom I was the center of the universe, immediately became more overprotective. Because both women were and still are very conscious of and obsessed with their image in the eyes of others, they forbade me to leave the house at any time without my head covered up, and any mention of my hair loss in public was prohibited. Because we were dealing with an unknown entity in terms of what was causing my hair loss and what could be done about it, my mother and grandmother initially decided upon using scarves to cover up the baldness.

I honestly cannot say that I recall being teased or picked on during those first years.

However, with the intuition only a child can have, I began to pick up the feeling that my baldness was something embarrassing to a lot of people, and that made me feel ashamed to be the cause of the embarrassment. I think those early feelings of shame and embarrassment – the need to hide my problem – coupled with my own natural talents and the desire to show them off were the catalysts that fueled my desire to be known for something other than my hair loss. So I threw myself into my schoolwork. I finished my homework assignments faster and more often than my older classmates, with very few or no errors.

Looking back on it now, I think it might have continued this way forever had it not been for a breakthrough and the intervention of some wonderful people.

The first day I wore my new wig to school I was very excited. Now that I looked just like everyone else, I could go about the business of just being a kid, not "a kid with some issues." As I was heading to chapel that first Monday morning, some of the students in the hallway stared, but I didn't realize it for what it was just yet. One or two students asked me if my hair had grown back over the holidays, and in my naïveté I proudly told them that no, I had gotten a wig so I could have hair just like them. I was answered with a strange look and suddenly I began to feel that maybe – just maybe – telling everyone that I had new hair might not have been the best idea. That feeling was justified as my class entered the chapel and took our usual seats in front. As we passed everyone, I heard their whispers and from the corner of my eye I saw some students pointing and even heard a snicker or two.

Even though my best friend at the time told me that everything was fine, I began to doubt her, especially when someone behind us said "Look, it's a wig!" It was at that moment that I felt true embarrassment and shame – embarrassed because apparently my wig very obviously looked like a wig (to a child's eyes) and shame because I had to wear the wig in the first place. Even now, more than 20 years later, I cannot recall this event without tears coming to my eyes and having to pause for a moment, because the shame and embarrassment was and is so overwhelming that my heart hurts to think about it. My reaction now is the same as my reaction then. I became very red-faced and hung my head, and quite sincerely wished that the floor would have opened up and swallowed me whole. I honestly don't recall the rest of the chapel service that first morning, but I do know that I would not have made it through that service without my friend holding my hand and reassuring me that everything would be fine.

Obviously, school was more difficult than my parents had imagined. Unfortunately, I couldn't stop that unhappiness from carrying over into my home life as well. I stopped going outside with my sisters and chose to keep myself in my room with my books. I stopped asking to go places with my grandmother, my aunts and uncles, even my parents. If my parents wanted to go somewhere, the first question I asked was if I had to wear my wig or cover my head. If the answer was yes, then I didn't want to go. This meant that I hardly went anywhere unless I had to, because my mother's answer to that question was ALWAYS yes. When my brother was born, my joy at having a baby brother was tempered by the fear that I had to go out in public and expose my head. My way around that was to convince my grandmother to take my sisters and me to the hospital at night, before visiting hours ended, so I saw as few people as possible. My sisters started to complain that I never wanted to play with them or anyone else, and after awhile the neighbors presumed that my parents had only three children instead of 4, because I simply disappeared. At school, however, I was totally different. My classmates teased me, picked on me, and generally bullied me to no end; however, I basked in the glow of academic achievement. I lived my life for each and every academic contest that I entered, whether it be essay writing, speech giving, general quiz bowl knowledge, you name it – I found a way to enter the contest and not only win, but completely destroy my competition.

During these difficult years, one person who remained my constant friend and companion and taught me more about acceptance and self-worth than anyone I ever knew. That person was my father, Michael. My father was a bookish sort, like me. Raised in California's foster care system off and on throughout his childhood, and separated from his sisters for much of that time, he understood my feelings of loneliness and isolation during those years. My father, always a gentle-hearted, generous man, and with the protectiveness of any father, absorbed my pain as his own and often went out of his way to make sure that he didn't treat me any differently than anyone else. His approach to this was a study of contrasts. Where my mother and grandmother always insisted on my keeping my head covered when going out in public, my father would ask me what I wanted to wear. If I said that I wanted to go bare-headed, then he would accept that decision without question and we would go on our way. If someone chose to stare a little too long, he would ask them if they wanted to ask me something and wait for an answer. This prompted me to tell the gawker about alopecia, what it did, and that of course, it was impolite to stare for too long without getting the facts. When we went on school field trips, my father was always the classroom parent, going just as much to experience the joy of field trips he never got to take in his own childhood as he was to keep me company. My most memorable field trip I ever took with my father was to the Masterworks art exhibit at the Tennessee State Museum in 1990. This collection, from the Bridgestone Museum of Art in Tokyo, Japan, houses hundreds of priceless works of art by Monet, Manet, Pissarro, Renoir, Degas, Picasso, Rembrandt, Raphael, Van Gogh, Reubens, and others considered to be the most remarkable artists in history. We spent hours perusing each and every one of the paintings, discussing what we liked the most about the paintings. That one day I spent with my father I will always cherish, for it seemed like a culmination of the lessons he taught me about decision-making, self-reliance, and respect for others. My father was the one who laid the foundation for what to look for in a romantic relationship. He was the one who gave me the traditional "birds and the bees" talk, and was the first person to present the possible reality that AA could possibly be something I would live with for the rest of my life. Although he also didn't focus on this, he wanted me to be prepared on how to deal with my AA when I hit puberty and all its changes.

It was very interesting to enter high school with a head full of long, dark hair. (After all those years of drugs and treatments my hair was almost black instead of the blonde my BA pictures showed.) Most of the students that I had gone to school with actually did not recognize me with hair, and their first and unanimous question was, "Is that hair yours??" Actually, truth be told, high school with hair – to me, anyway – was a lot less traumatic than it was for a lot of people. Once my hair grew back, the worst I had to worry about in school was whether or not someone was trying to be my friend to get the homework answers or because they thought I was cool.

I won't say I was the most popular person in school during those years, because I definitely wasn't. However, once I stopped caring about whether or not I fit in with everyone, I did notice a substantial increase in my popularity amongst my peers. Was it because I wasn't trying so hard to be liked? Was it because of my hair? During my junior and the first half of my senior year, I relaxed enough to not let my hair be the driving force in my life. I colored my hair for the first time, and I almost believed that my hair would never fall out again.

It is a dangerous thing to grow up with less-than-realistic expectations, and it can be devastating when the reality of your expectations is significantly less than what you planned. I found this lesson out in the spring of 1995, when I discovered that dreaded spot. A single spot that caused the world to fall out from under my feet. Surprisingly enough, I wasn't scared or nervous, or even alarmed that my hair was falling out again. What was bothersome, though, was the speed with which my hair fell out this time. When my hair initially fell out at age 4, it took nearly a year for it to be totally gone.

This time, it was gone completely by June. In May, when I graduated from high school, I had blended my hair into a wig to disguise my hair loss.

I will never forget the day I shaved my head for the first time. It was on a Saturday morning, about 9am. I woke up before everyone else, and I don't know what prompted me to make the decision to shave my head. All I know is that I went outside to take a walk, and when I stopped walking, I was in front of the barber shop a few blocks up the street. I asked the barber to cut my hair off with a straight razor, and when the barber finished, I put a bandana on my head and walked back home. By the time I got home, everyone was up and moving. So, not to be subtle about it, I walked into the house, said, "BOY, it's hot outside!" and swept off the bandana. Everyone freaked out! I think I spent the entire day with everyone in the household rubbing my head and just looking – it wasn't because I was bald, because everyone was used to that – rather; it was because I had willingly removed my hair instead of letting alopecia take the last few strands. The first time I shaved my head represented the first time I exerted control over my appearance and how I felt about myself, and I have tried to maintain that control since then.

In the 13 years since I shaved my head for the first time, I have lived with long periods of full re-growth, and longer periods of total baldness.

This latest period of loss, I believe, was triggered by the sudden, traumatic death of my beloved father in January 2002. At the time of his death, I was 23 years old. My father, whose calm demeanor and cool intellect was my rock during the darkest years of my childhood, was my best friend. I could talk to my father about anything, and he would listen without being judgmental, offer his advice on how to handle the situation, and trust me to make the right decision regarding the situation.

Most important of all, he was the constant buffer between my mother and me. When her controlling tendencies and over-protectiveness pushed me to the brink of losing my temper, many times it was his intervention that prevented all-out warfare.

In the years since then, I have had very brief periods of partial re-growth, but never the total re-growth I had enjoyed in the years immediately before my father's death. In a sense, I wear my baldness as a lasting mark of my grief and sorrow at losing my best friend. The death of a parent, especially an untimely death, is not something from which any child ever recovers. I'm no exception.

Since becoming an adult, I find myself in the unique position of coming across former classmates who either never knew about my alopecia, or were some of my biggest bullies and tormentors when we were in school. Usually, they run into my mother or my sister, and prostrate themselves with apologies for the way they treated me all those years ago. I have received several apologies personally, and while I accept them all graciously, I can't help but be a bit ambivalent about them as well. From my parents and my grandmother, I learned about the healing power of forgiveness alongside those lessons of right and wrong that every child learns. By the time I had become an adult, I had forgiven most, of the people who had picked on me in my childhood as well as the adults who had rejected me as a grown woman. By receiving these apologies, the door that was formerly closed had merely been opened again, and as an adult, it is increasingly difficult to close that door again. Perhaps it is this repression of all the anger and sadness I felt as a child that has led me to seek out other alopecians as an adult.

So how has alopecia affected me throughout my life? Simply put, it has molded me into a shrewd, intelligent, gregarious woman, yet it has also made me a more empathetic person. I truly identify with the suffering of others, and go out of my way not to hurt the feelings of anyone with the words that I say, because having been the victim of hurtful words during the most vulnerable periods of my life, I truly would not wish that pain on my worst enemy. But AA has also blessed me with an amazing strength to withstand almost any crisis, and made me fiercely protective of my independence. AA is a double-edged sword; it alternately blesses and curses everyone whose life it touches. It changes and transforms us and presents us with a new reality. I told my story once upon a time ago, when I was 11 years old. I am telling my story again, nearly 20 years later, to remind the world that yes, I live with AA. But I am still here. I am still living, still thriving, and in spite of AA.

$\mathcal{S}$elf Confidence

Anna Fitzpatrick
New Zealand
Alopecia Universalis

When I first started losing my hair my mum and dad thought I was cutting my hair like I would do with my Barbie dolls. Then one eyebrow fell out and it became obvious that there was something wrong.

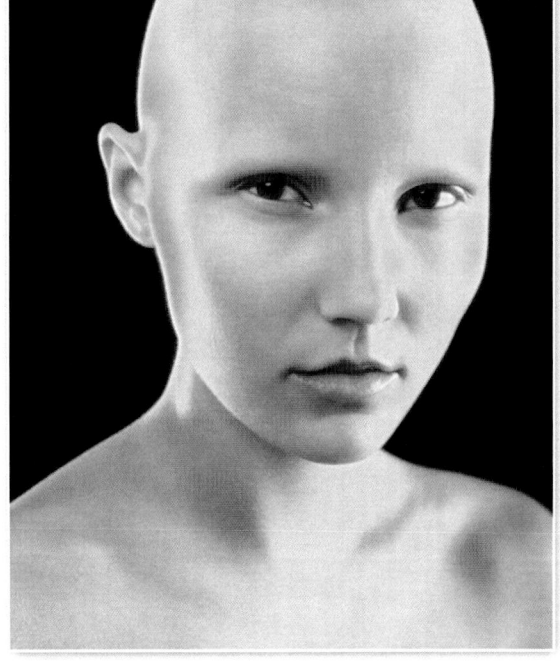

But I think now that losing it at a younger age was much easier than if it had happened in my teenage years. I had a longer time to learn to accept my self and my lack of hair before I started worrying about what I looked like for the opposite sex. The only comment I remember that upset me at the time was that I looked like someone's bald gran-dad.

At my year 6 camp I was having a great time. I had had my new wig from freedom hair for about a year and I could finally join in with the other kids swinging upside down and going on the mud/water slide.

The first time I went down the slide it was great, so I ran to the top for another turn. On this last slide my wig flew off at the bottom as it was slightly too small for me and the back was sitting quite high at the back of my head. The water pressure got under it and it went flying. I knew it had come off, as I was underwater at the end of the slide. I held my breath for as long as I could so I wouldn't have to come up and face the hundreds of kids around the slide. It was one of the worst days of my life. My secret was out and I surfaced to a mixture of shocked/horrified faces and laughs from the boys who regularly teased me. I think everyone knew I wore a wig at this stage but it was a shock for them to have there suspicions confirmed and to see me bare.

Everyone accepted it after year 8 and I had a really amazing group of friends who supported me and never let one single person get away with being mean to me again. I have to say that one or two of these girls who are still my best friends were some of the girls who originally teased me, but they realized that it was terrible of them and realised it was there immaturity that lead them to it.

During the age of 13 and 14 I had been asked to join numerous modeling agencies but I never took it seriously until I was out for dinner for a friend's birthday

and a woman sat down next to me and started talking to me about it. I agreed to go into the agency and have some pictures taken.

I met the owner and she took me under her wing and put me on the books. They had not realized I had no hair they just thought I had an unusual edgy look with no eyebrows that would work really well in NZ. As soon as I told them I had alopecia they were very excited. They asked if I would model bald and I was hesitant at first and said it would depend on the circumstances.

It's funny what the title model does for you; I went from Anna the "bald girl" to Anna "the model". I suddenly was a lot more popular. Modeling boosted my self-confidence and helped me become the person I am today. I ended up on a billboard bald proving you don't need hair and to be conventionally

good looking to be beautiful.

Alopecia can be an emotionally crippling disease. I know this from first hand experience, as would all other suffers in the world. But we can grow and become beautiful, strong and confident men and women. The first step to this is to help grow awareness through the communities of Alopecia. So that those comments of disgust I heard when I was a child can be eradicated.

www.princesscharlottealopecia.com

Living Joyously

Annette Moore
United States
Cicatricial Alopecia and Alopecia Totalis

I was diagnosed with two types of alopecia. Cicatricial Central Centrifugal Alopecia (CCCA) and Alopecia Totalis.

In the beginning, it was extremely difficult to accept and there were others who found it difficult to accept the way that I looked. I found out very early in my journey that it was not going to be a straight line to acceptance. I had such a horrible self image disconnect. At my lowest point, I couldn't even look in the mirror. I felt so ashamed of my hair loss and did everything to hide it from others.

It became too heavy of a burden to hide my look, my shame, and my guilt amongst other negative feelings I was experiencing. It was then I decided that it just didn't make that much sense to put that much emphasis on my hair. My hair, or lack there of doesn't define who I am. It doesn't define what positivity and beauty exists inside my heart and mind.

Being stripped of what many people feel is a symbol of health, beauty and status has caused me to examine what really lies beneath my surface. I've learned so much about myself throughout this experience. In the beginning what seemed to be like a curse has now turned into not one, but many beautiful blessings.

In my life I've come to a place of "self empowerment" through "self acceptance." Being a woman and having no hair doesn't have to be a negative experience.

I am here now, this is my journey and the people who love and care about me don't care that I am bald. I love my new crown. I'd like to say that I have been hereby, Crowned Regal.

www.crownedregal.com

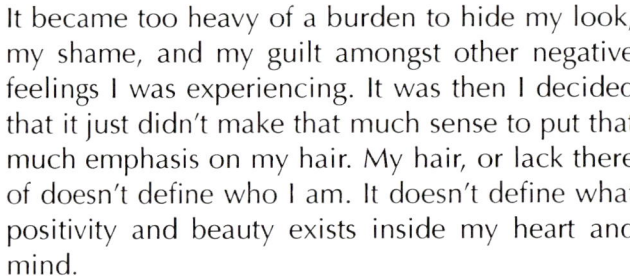

Overcoming

Dotty Jenkins
United States
Alopecia Totalis

In retrospect, losing all my hair is nothing compared to finding out that the man I married molested my daughter. I put the monster in jail, and tried to be strong.

I started to notice small patches of hair missing in October of 2001. The patches were increasing in size and quantity, and by February of 2002, I had lost most of the hair on the top of my head. I was able to wear a bandana and still at least look "normal" to everyone else. I did a whole gambit of medical treatments to no avail, I even tried Chiropractic and Naturopathic medicine and still nothing. But, waking up every morning with a pillow full of hair and seeing huge clumps of my hair in the drain every time I took a shower was too much for me to take. I decided it would be better for me to shave what little hair I had left off and wear a wig.

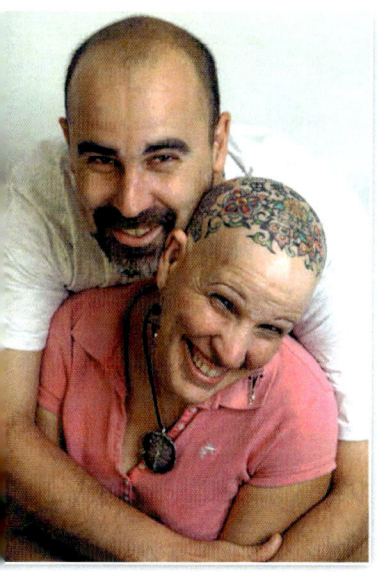

So there I was a 39 year old bald woman!!! I didn't like to look in the mirror as I hated the way I looked. How was anyone ever going to love me again??? Who was going to want to deal with that?? I went through the dating scene, telling the men up front about my hair loss. Most of them would say it didn't bother them but it really did, and I wouldn't get a call back. Until I met Brett.

There are more Alopecia sufferers than anyone realizes because a lot of them suffer in silence, thinking that they are the only ones. Some don't even come out of their homes if they can't afford a decent wig. Society puts so much emphasis on looks, and that makes people afraid to be different. I am different, and I don't care!!! I can wear my wig and nobody even gives me a second glance but if I was to walk out my door without a head covering, people stare!! It's human nature. I tattooed my head so that I would stand out and people would ask questions. I take that opportunity to educate them about Alopecia and assure them that I don't have cancer (which is the first assumption that people make!!).

I hope that more Alopecians can stand up and be proud of who they are. I am still me.....

om Paved the Way

Andrea Roussel
United States
Alopecia Universalis

I credit my "okay- ness" partly to my God given personality, but also to my family's reaction. I'm sure watching your two year olds hair fall out and not know why is a scary thing, but I am also sure my parents' absorbed much of the scared, sad, 'why me' feelings for me. I never felt those feelings in reference to my hair. I was never treated differently by anyone in my family.

The Bible tells us that God will give us nothing we cannot stand up underneath. While I may have not been given hair I was given an incredibly strong, intelligent mother. I have not stood up underneath the trial of being bald alone.

My grade school years...

Putting my hair on each day was like putting on a shoe. It's just what I did. At my young age, I was not quite strong enough to push the hair piece on. My solution? A head stand! Before school I would kick my feet up against the wall and let the floor push the hair on. Ironically, I did this so much I wore a bald spot in the mold.

During a trip to the post office with my mom, the post man said, "I like your big red bow." To my mom and the post man's surprise I replied, while pulling my hair off, "do you like my fake hair too?" That post man still says a special hello to me when I visit Massachusetts.

When I was a junior in high school I decided to stop wearing my hair while playing sports. I would wear my hair to school then take it off before practice. After graduating from high school I attended the University of Louisville where I played field hockey. Nothing changed on my end. I never wore my hair while playing. It is a neat experience to play on a college team with people from all over the world. I would say having alopecia made me fit in more because in reality everyone has something. Louisville Field Hockey boasted no hair, eyes that twitched an allergy to wheat, toes that pointed in, haunting pasts, rainods, capped teeth and many other abnormalities that really just made us all normal.

During college I met my now boyfriend. When he was first going to come watch me play field hockey I told him I had alopecia so he wouldn't wonder where I was when he showed up and didn't see a red head on the field.

I remember someone asking me, "Does your boyfriend know? What does he say?" As if MY GOODNESS! YOU'RE ACTUALLY TELLING ME A BOY THINKS YOU ARE BEAUTIFUL WITHOUT HAIR! These sorts of questions honestly puzzle me. What kind of relationship would it be if he did not know or if he did not think I was beautiful? A superficial one is the answer. I think should I sarcastically respond, "Well, he says, as long as I look at you from the neck down then we'll have a great future together."

I figure God has a sense of humor because my roommate is a hair dresser. She recently told me about a hair piece that stays on the head permanently. I debated about moving forward with getting the hair piece for a few reasons. I could not decide weather or not the cost of the hair piece was worth it considering I am okay with being bald, and I have my molds which serve their purpose. My mom and boyfriend like to see and kiss my bald head. I wondered if I would miss being able to take my hair off and see my shiny head. I also felt like a hypocrite. Was I being myself if I got a hair piece that made it so I would never be bald? A discussion with my roommate made me realize. Having the hair piece does not change the fact that I am comfortable being bald or change who I am. If there came a day that I could no longer afford the new hair piece I would go back to my molds and baldness without missing a beat. This reminded me of when my hair began to grow back.

In my last year in college my hair began growing in like a baby's peach fuzz, after a janitor prayed for me. It grew enough that I could no longer wear my molds because the stubble broke the suction. When the hair was no longer than a man's five o'clock shadow, I joked with my friend that I had bed head (it was the truth

though!). Around the same time, my mom got me a little bottle of hair spray so my hair would not get in my eyes during a field hockey game, even though it was no where near long enough to do so. My hair grew for a year. It looked just like my mom's, with curls and all.

During that time, I remember walking down the street with my boyfriend holding his hand. I was wearing athletic shorts and a t-shirt. A truck drove by and the passenger screamed, "FAG!" This was the first time I cried because of a comment someone made. It was wrong on so many levels. I suppose it is my Achilles' heel. I do not like being mistaken for a boy!

Continuing on with the positives of my hair growing, because the Janitor prayed and my hair grew soon after, a Christian show got wind of my story. The day I was interviewed for the show I noticed a spot in the TV monitor. I had gotten a spot earlier that year that grew back. I wondered if this one would do the same. It didn't. As the rest of my hair got longer, this spot got bigger. The spot looked just like the spot I had seen on a home video of me at about age four, not too long before. I thought of when I was watching the video and saying to my mom...

"Look at that spot, mom!

Why didn't you just shave it all off?"

Having to make the decision that it was time to shave the rest of the hair off because it just was not healthy hair any more was not easy. As okay with my baldness as I am, of course I would love to have my own natural hair grow. Of course I want the latest hair styles and to do all the girly hair stuff. I shaved the hair off one year after it began to grow.

I still believe it was an answer to a prayer. I got to see that my hair was the same as my mom's. I got to share a story that shows prayers are answered today. I got to feel the wind blow through natural hair. I got to feel what my mom must have felt when faced with the decision of shaving her young daughter's hair off.

If my natural hair grows back and falls out again, if I have a hair piece that I take on and off or if I have a hair piece that stays on permanently I am me. I know I can walk around with a bald or hairy head held high.

I have always believed I am bald for a reason. I have learned though that I am bald for many reasons. I have got to see my mom fight so hard to make sure I never went without. I have got to hear a grade school boy stick up for his best girl friend. I have got to help a middle school girl go through her own hair loss. I have been able to unknowingly show people that there are much worse things than not having hair. I have been able to experience a relationship where my beautiful sister looked at me no differently than she looked at anyone else and never made fun of me, even in siblings arguments. I have been able to know that my boyfriend feels real love for me, too. I am blessed enough to know what it feels like to be loved unconditionally and feel true comfort in a relationship.

As an elementary school teacher now, I am able to tell five hundred children a year that it really is a person character that matters and that we all have differences. I am able to teach them that not everyone who is bald has cancer. I have been able to be different and stand out. I have been able to know what it is to be starred at and be fine. I have been able to be starred at and not feel fine, but be stronger. I have been reminded that I do have a story and I was able to tell it to you.

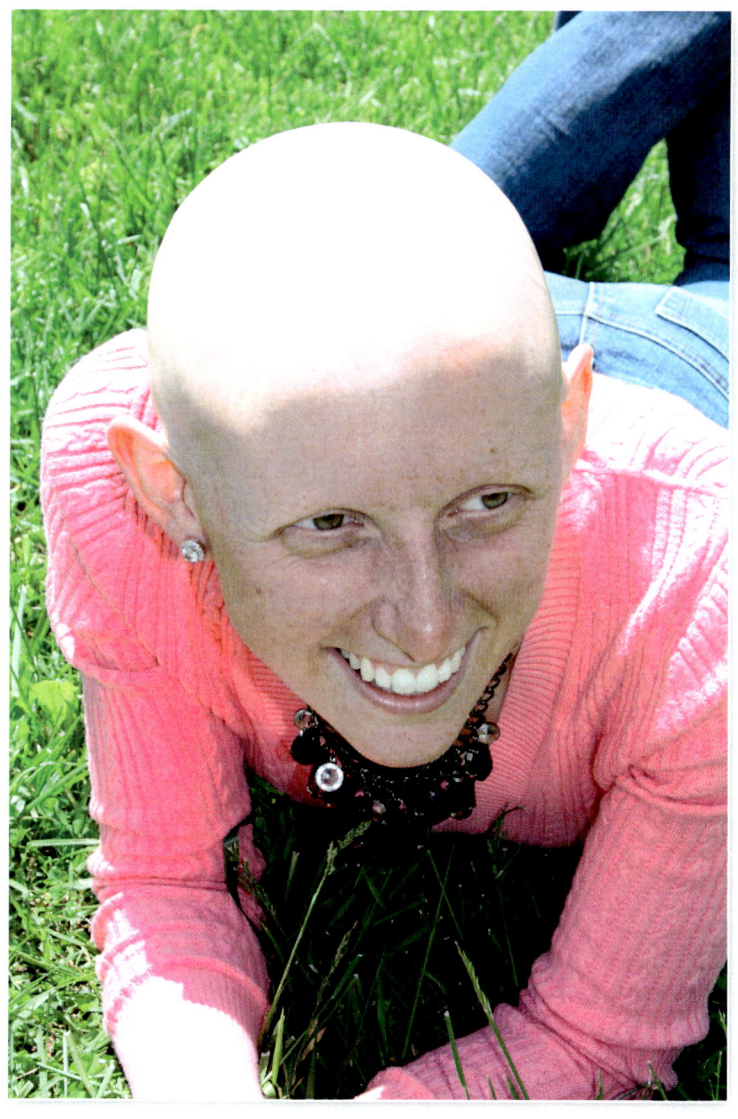

Feeling Free
Jill Cook
United States
Alopecia Areata

I was 8 years old. I was none the wiser. To me, the spots didn't really matter. They could be easily covered up with a pony tail and nobody could even see them. The hair eventually grew back and I went on with my life.

My hair stayed around until about my sophomore year in high school. Alopecia, then, reared its ugly head again and this time with a vengeance. It took all my arm and leg hair, most my eyebrows and two triangle shaped areas along the front of my scalp. This time, it was a much bigger deal. What was I gonna do? What were my friends gonna say? Was my hair ever gonna come back?

High school ended and my head full of hair remained. College started and my life was wonderful. It remained that way right until finals started my freshman year. The overwhelming stress triggered my alopecia once again. Once again, my eyebrows disappeared and so did the same hair on my scalp. Once again, I headed to the dermatologist to get shots in my head. The hair eventually returned on its own time.

College is really where the vicious cycle started. Anytime I was really stressed out, the hair fell out. It always came back, but there was always an underlying fear that it wouldn't. I got comfortable with the way things were and how I looked.

College ended and I was hoping with that so would the cycle. However, I was accepted into vet school and the stress was inevitable. It didn't take long to realize that my hair wasn't going to stick around long. By the middle of my freshman year, the spots were bigger than they had ever been. I was lucky if I had one eyebrow hair. This was a whole new battle for me. I suddenly wasn't comfortable with the way that I looked anymore. I was self-conscious about my bald spots and was afraid that they were showing all the time. I very carefully arranged my hair everyday to cover the spots up. I made sure that on the outside everything was fine, regardless of how I felt on the inside.

The middle of my sophomore year, I met the most amazing man and fell in love with him. I was honest from the start about my disease and the devastating effects it could have by taking ALL my hair. He didn't care. He gave me the strength not to care either. He was the one that I eventually asked to shave my head. I got to the point where I thought I would feel better just being bald than trying to hide my spots all the time. Having my head shaved was a very interesting experience! Never have I felt so free and so scared at the same time. I walked beside the mirror and didn't recognize myself anymore.

I've been bald now for 3 years. I have never been more comfortable with the way that I feel about myself. I know I look different than everyone else but I'm okay with that. My hair has eventually filled in and I only have one small spot left.

People may ask, "Why haven't you just let your hair grow out now that you know you can?" and my response?

"Because Bald is Beautiful!"

Self Reflection

New Blooms

Little Girls Living with Alopecia

Learning How to Fly

Small yet eager
The baby bird cries.
She leaps from the nest,
Spreads her wings and flies.

A turbulent take-off,
Balance growing steady.
She wouldn't have jumped,
If she wasn't ready.

A loop and a twirl,
Experience makes us strong!
It takes a mistake,
To learn when you are wrong.

When you're having a bad day,
Remember that baby bird.
It takes a lot of patience
To become who you will be ...
Or so I've heard!

Carol Jones

Daddy's Heart

Kiah
United States
Alopecia Unversalis

Kiah began to loose her hair when she was about 3 years old. We first noticed that something was going on when those little bald circles that are so familiar to everyone in the Alopecia world, began to show up. It was a tough time for our family, and there were a lot of changes going on. Kiah's Alopecia started around the time that her mother Kerri and I were splitting up. While she was young, it was clear that moving out of the house that we shared took a toll on Kiah and her sister Kaycee, as it would any child. It was decided that I would take primary custody of the children and that we would move back in to my parent's house while I finished up my Masters Program and began my PhD. The adjustment was difficult for all of us but me and the girls found strength in each other and after a period of sadness, we became more comfortable with the idea that we were all still a family, but the structure or our family had changed. Thinking back, I have heard that stress might be a trigger that sets off Alopecia, and I will always wonder if that stressful time may have been a factor in Kiah's development of Alopecia.

The following year, Kiah's hair began to fall out rapidly. At the time I had never heard of the condition, so being the researcher that I am, I immediately sought to find out all I could about AA. I was relieved to find out that it was not a life threatening condition and that her physical health would not be affected. Earlier that year, during a hot, humid summer, Kiah had a couple of bouts of what I thought could be asthma and I was fearful that the two were related and symptoms of a larger health problem. Luckily, she has not had any relapses of the asthma like symptoms and as we found out, the reason her hair was falling out was because of AA. The dermatologist was hesitant to prescribe a treatment because of Kiah's young age. She recommended that we wait for about a month or so and check back to see how the spots had progressed.

When it was time to schedule a new appointment I had taken a job as graduate research assistant at UW-Milwaukee and had a different insurance plan which required a change in dermatologist. The new dermatologist confirmed that it was indeed AA and gave us a prescription for two topical treatments. We used both but her hair continued to fall out and when it became clear that the treatments were having no effect we stopped using them. Kiah was not particularly thrilled with the routine of having to apply foam and liquid to her head 2x daily anyway, so we stopped using them. Within a year from the first diagnosis all of Kiah's hair had fallen out. In some ways it was sort of a relief for all her hair to fall out because, as a single dad, I had no idea how to work with the patches of hair on her head. I've had very short hair the majority of my life and now I only have about 1/2 of my own hair left myself! All of Kiah's hair had fallen out about four to six months prior to the start of her first day of K4. We were all a little nervous because we didn't know how the other kids would treat her. Luckily, we had some experience in dealing with this issue from Kiah's time in daycare.

The start of the 2007-2008 school year was going to be a new experience for both of my daughters, my oldest, Kaycee, was transferring schools. Since Kaycee was starting out in a new place as well, I was worried that she would not be in as good of a position to able to support her and defend her sister as I had hoped. In addition, the school I was sending them too was a school where all subjects are taught in about 80% Spanish. New school, new language, and the challenges of having Kiah feel comfortable in a different setting with new kids unfamiliar to her condition. It was a lot to take in, and we were unsure how it would all turn out.

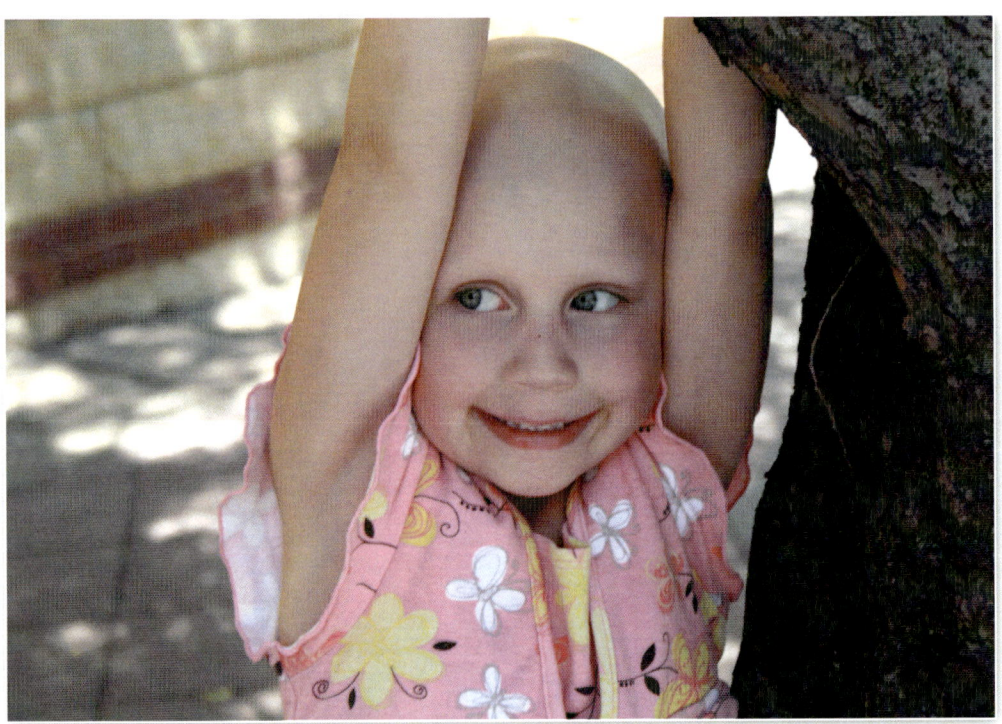

Prior to the start of the school year, I spoke with both the administration and Kiah's K-4 teacher. Both assured me that the school was a very supportive and made up of a diverse body of students with many different backgrounds. In essence, the school has all types of children, and Kiah, with her Alopecia, would just be another one of them. That was exactly what I wanted to hear.

Soon after school started, I approached the teacher (with Kiah's permission) and brought her the book about a little girl with Alopecia so she could read it to the class during story time. The book really helped the class and the teacher understand a lot more about Alopecia.

Currently, the only hairs that Kiah has remaining are her eyelashes (which are beginning to fall out) and a small patch on one leg. Once it became clear that Kiah had Alopecia Universalis, we realized that the likelihood that her hair would grow back on its own was greatly decreased. As a family, we are ok with that. It's hard at this point to imagine Kiah with hair for a variety of reasons. We have a ritual where I kiss the top of her baldhead before bed every night. Everyone comments on how cute she is with her floppy hats, and how her lack of hair just makes her big blue eyes stand out that much more. Mornings for me are tough enough trying to brush her sister's hair. I sometimes struggle with one ponytail (I am getting better), but while Kaycee is crying about me brushing her hair and it hurting, Kiah gets a chuckle that she doesn't have to worry about that. I'll admit, I kind of like it too, doing little girls hair is just not something I am good at!

Kiah, and our family have received so much support that AU has in a sense been a blessing for us. While we are not together, her mother and I have become much more conscious of the way we deal with each other and the girls, making sure that we do everything we can to place our full support behind them both. We have had a unified voice in giving Kiah's options such as wigs and hats, but making sure that she knows that going bald and presenting herself as she is, is Ok too.

Attending the Alopecia Conference was an unbelievable experience. As soon as we got to Louisville and began seeing all the other kids with Alopecia, Kiah just began to glow. She was a little shy at first, but she quickly made it known how excited she was. You could tell that she felt a sense of joy, and relief, that she was not alone. When we got back to the hotel room after the attending a baseball game with the conference Kiah said, " I never knew there were so many Alopecia kids daddy!" I must admit, neither did I! The whole conference was fantastic. Both the girls and I made new friends, and had experiences that we will never forget. As a family, we all felt a sense of closeness because we were all there supporting Kiah, and I like to think that Kiah felt that extra burst of love as well. For me, the conference was an emotional experience. For the first time ever, I got to see my daughter take off her hat in public. It took her a couple days, but she did it. When I saw her little bald head running around with her sister and her new friends, with reckless abandon, not worried about her hat falling off, my eyes may have watered up a bit.

I am sure that the future will bring new challenges for Kiah, especially when she gets older and begins to feel the increased pressure to fit in and present herself a certain way. But I am also sure that Kiah, and the rest of our family, will be able to meet these challenges head on. Seeing diverse types of people of all different age groups living with their Alopecia adds to our confidence and reminds us that many other people are dealing with the same issues, and overcoming them. I know that each new challenge will test Kiah, but also make her stronger and help her continue to blossom into the amazing person I know she will be.

$\mathcal{S}$cotlyn
United States
Alopecia Areata

It was 5 months prior to Scotlyn's 7th birthday when I noticed her biggest spot. "I didn't see it there yesterday", I said to myself. I was so puzzled and also scared that this was really happening to her.

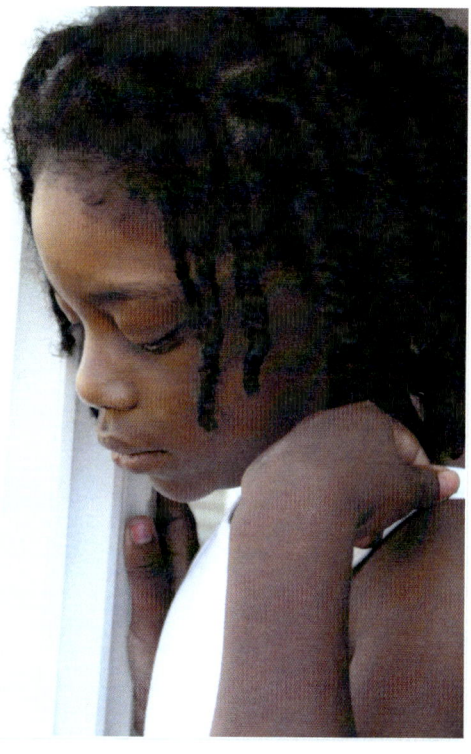

I called my husband in so he could see this very big, very smooth spot in her head. We just looked at one another not saying too much. Scotlyn then asked us what was wrong and I told her that she has a bald spot in her head. I handed her the mirror because she said that she wanted to see the spot. She was quiet as she looked at the spot and then said in a calm voice, "well I guess I have Alopecia just like you".

I never put two and two together. When Scotlyn was a baby, she had very small spots that would come and go. I never thought anything of it. Even when I was going through my hair loss, I never imagined that my little girl could have this condition, too.

So there's a possibility here that she may loose her hair and she may not, but I wanted to make sure that her feelings were not dismissed. I wanted to know what was on her mind. We as parents often assume that we know what our children are feeling, we jump to conclusion. I didn't want to conclude that just because I was okay with my hair loss and since she was around me…that she would be okay too.

So I asked her what she felt about this whole Alopecia thing.

"It was surprising mommy; I thought my hair was going to fall out like yours" she said.

She then said quietly, "I'll be sad if it ever were to all come out".

Scotlyn's spot has since grown back in. As I continue to become educated about the condition, I inform her about it too. I do this to empower her, and not to build doubt where she's self conscience and or paranoid about her appearance.

My advice to parents is put your child in the mirror at a very early age and teach them positive affirmations about their body image, their features, and their fingers and toes…nose and mouth. This experience with my child has taught me that kids do indeed soak up what they see their parents do. However, she never saw me in mirror on those days when I was telling myself how much I loved my teeth, even the crooked one or how much appreciate my bald head and lessons that it's teaching me. I love my body; I just need to make sure it stays healthy through eating right and exercising.

I truly believe that when your child see themselves in a positive light; it makes for an awesome start toward building a healthy self esteem, and the power to keep their head up despite what anyone else thinks or says about them.

-Julia

*D*emeiah
United States
Alopecia Unversalis

Midori
United States
Alopecia Unversalis

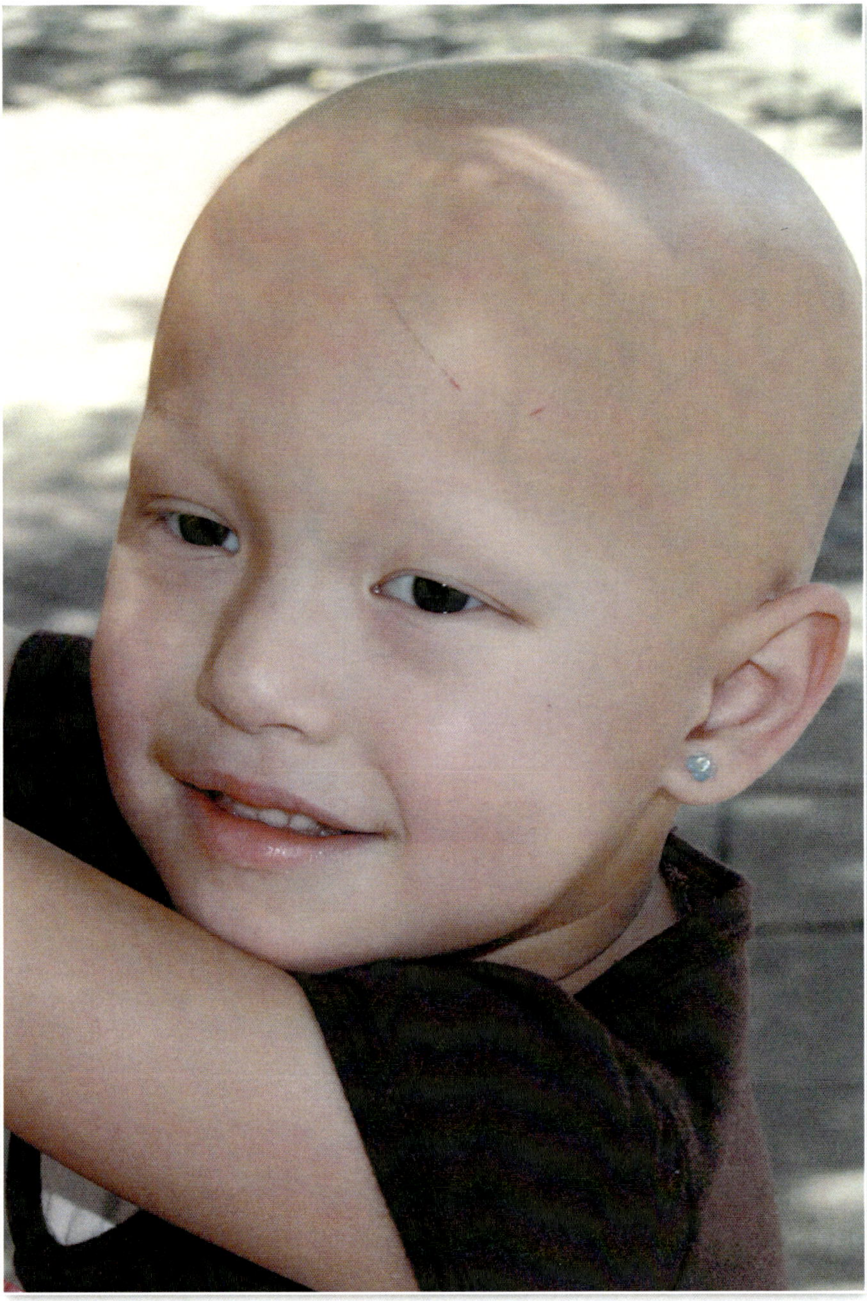

*Just Love
Anthéa
France
Alopecia Unversalis

Anthéa is 6 years old and a very funny, intelligent little girl with a strong personality. She often will asks when her hairs are going to grow again…I've no answer.

Anthéa is surrounded well by family. Her older brother takes charge well of her even if they often bicker.

The only advice I have to give is to be a good listener and give a lot of love.

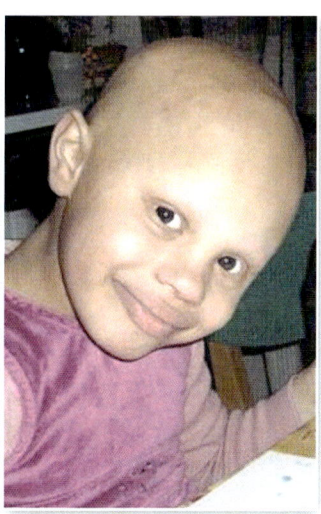

Self Reflection

ℳetamorphosis: Final Thought

As I have moved through the stages of alopecia, I often wonder if I've experienced them all. There has been sadness and grief, false hope, renewed strength and now acceptance of the things I cannot change. I know that it is possible that my hair may start growing tomorrow, but I'm not holding my breath. I have no sense of anticipation, or expectations that the lovely hair I used to have will be part of my reflection when I look in the mirror. This doesn't mean that I've given up. It just means that I accept what has been given to me. I know that there are hurdles and even more hills to climb, but I look forward to experiencing what these changes will bring.

Deeann Graham
Alopecia Universalis

The Purpose of Journaling?

It is very important to find a moment in your day to write and reflect on you. This could be about your feelings on life, love, family, friends and most importantly YOU!

When dealing with Alopecia or any other type of life changing issue, writing in a journal, you're able to capture your true essence and deepest thought. The goal is that you are true to yourself as you put pen to paper.

Hopefully one day you'll find yourself looking back at your words and seeing just how far you've come, how you've grown and how you've come to really appreciate your destiny.

Julia's Journal Entry

September 6, 2008

I woke up this morning unaware that it would be an emotional one.

This morning, it was gloomy outside from the remnants of the hurricane. However, I got up with a mission.

I needed to go to the store to get my son something to wear for his cousin's sweet 16 birthday party and I was going to pick up my grandmother from the nursing home.

When I finally got out of the bed, I walked into the bathroom and looked into the mirror. I got this glimpse of a head that hadn't been shaven in 5 days.

By the third day I just chalked it up to being lazy. On the fourth day I threw a cap on my head because I was being totally lazy and with the hair growth my spots on the side and in the back of my head were really showing. Today the fifth day was different…

I'm going to the barbershop!

I knew that I still had a few spots in the back and on the side of my head, but I can get them faded and have a nice haircut, is what you were telling yourself. OR, I could just shave it off. I mean how long will you stay this time hair?

Why the Confusion today Julia…

So I made up in my mind that I was going to the barbershop and quickly got dressed, put make-up on and truly felt that this was what I needed to do for me. I mean these are the phases of Alopecia and I'm always talking about "Change".

I saw D on the way out and told him what I was going to do. It's funny because he looked at me as I was explaining to him why I was going to do this, as if to say whatever woman, do what you have to do. I appreciate D and how supportive he has always been when it came to my hair loss. Today, I am grateful and thank God for my husband!

So I've made up in my mind that I was going to go to get my fade, I'm going to see just how long my hair is going to grow.

As I was on my way to the ATM to withdraw some money in order to pay the barber, I was talking to myself the whole way there.

"Will people think that I'm real?"

"Will I still be representing Alopecia?"

As I continued to talk to myself the more confusing my thoughts got. My main question was, "WHY?"

Why was it coming back now? I'm comfortable with who I am with no hair now. It was almost like I was SCARED! Scared of my hair coming back, how silly is that? Most people want their hair to come back, I mean isn't that the goal Julia?

It was funny because when I withdrew the money I noticed that I conveniently got stopped by each red light and each time I would change my mind.

So of course my mind starts to wander and I was trying to figure out who I should be calling for support and this is how I would like to remember this phone call...

"Hello, Nettie"

I was thinking about this person and how she is always so uplifting, ever since the first phone call. We've never met face to face, but she's my sister from a far and it's like we've known each other for such a long time.

In her joyous voice as always, she said "Hey Sweetie, how are you?"

"I'm confused and a little emotional", I answered

So I tell her what's going on in the life of "No Hair, NOW hair".

"Ain't this about some stuff!" I pictured her putting her had on her hip when she said that.

She went on to say basically that we've accepted this life changing condition and now that we're in the arena of uplifting and helping others deal with the affects, it seems for some reason we're trying to be blocked from doing so.

She too had something going on with her beautiful "Crown" at the time as well. She told me to rock my bald head, and be proud...

Some type of intervention was trying to happen, negative intervention because our call was disconnected. When I called back I got her voicemail so just left a message.

By this time I'd pulled up to the barbershop and I just sat there…waiting…for what? I don't know. Then I pulled the sun visor down and opened the mirror and I looked at myself.

"So what will you do?"

When I got out of the truck and entered the shop I had to make another call to Bibi. I told her that I was at the barbershop; of course she was surprised to hear that I was and asked me why I was there.

"I don't know, I'm confused", I started to fill up with emotion and started crying.

Bibi just said to me a week prior to this emotional event that she feels that when I go out with my bald head, she feels that I am at total comfort with me. I go out and this is it, it just is…

She goes on to say that I had two options and I can look at it two ways. I can say to my hair, "Hair, I really don't need you, I've been without you this long" and just shave it off like I've been doing. "Or" she said "you can call it out and say to my hair, ok hair let me see what you got! How long will you grow this time?" Call it out she said.

I thanked her for listening and hung up.

I thought to myself today about my mission. I raise questions as a bald woman because it's not normal to see a bald woman on any given day just in the grocery store, there are very few. I get the opportunity to educate others who can mustard up enough nerve to ask me about my bald head. A person responded to my blog "No Hair, Now Hair" saying that I didn't have to be the poster child of Alopecia and to just wear a shirt displaying Alopecia if my hair comes back and by doing so I can still educate.

So I sat there in the seat waiting my turn, my mind started to wander again. I thought about the little 10 year old girl down South; she'd lost her father. He found me on a well known networking site under the word "Alopecia" and even though my profile is set to private he saw my "bald head" profile photo and sent me a message. He told me about her having Alopecia, sent photos and soon I was able to speak to her, regularly. She is such a bright little girl and talking to her inspired me to keep doing what I do and that's to inspire others. Once she lost her daddy, which was unexpected and very sudden, I found out from her aunt that she lost the rest of her hair. I still tear up at the thought. I know deep down that this little girl is destined for great things…I pray that I'm around to see her change the world with her "light".

When I spoke to her and her other aunt…I asked her aunt how she was doing and what was she wearing on her head. She told me that she didn't want to wear anything; her aunt said that she told them that she wanted to be just like Miss Julia. Tears immediately came to my eyes, I was humbled.

I also thought about the comment that my 7 year old told me. One morning while I was getting dressed for work, she stopped in her tracks and looked at me and uttered the words, "Mom, I want to be bald just like you". Are you kidding me, did she realize that she just made my heart skip a beat.

I always said that I can handle being bald, but how will I help my own child deal with it her Alopecia? Well, she eased my wandering heart that ached each time I noticed a spot in her head. She's going to be just fine and so will I. I thought after she made that comment if my purpose was for her, was I getting her prepared for something? Only God knows!

So he called my name and as I was walking toward his chair to get in it, he asked me what I wanted for him to do.

I thought in that split second, how I wasn't confused or scared because my hair is coming back. I'm grateful today that I did experience hair on my head and I'm grateful today of all the people who were apart of my morning's emotional event. I'm glad that right now I've come to the conclusion that hair does not make me nor does a bald head!

But I feel that I have this purpose and I felt this ease come over me…I told him that it's not time yet…

"Shave it off!"

Gratitude:

I thank God for all the lessons that He's teaching me. I have to continue to listen to my inner spirit because I truly believe that it's actually God's voice. I am a child learning how to walk again, holding my Father's hand and counting on Him to not let me fall. I know at times He'll test me to see if I got it and let go of my hand, but I guess that is the only way I can learn. Falling from time to time but trusting that He'll be there to help me back to my feet.

So what was this all about today? Who am I, really?

Today was about my journey and its twist and turns, ups and downs. And who am I, really….I'm just Julia on a Mission!

elf Reflection Journal

"Discussing your Inner Thoughts"

Today _____/_____/_____

_____

_____

_____

_____

_____

_____

_____

_____

_____

_____

_____

_____

_____

_____

_____

_____

_____

_____

_____

_____

_____

_____

Today _____/_____/_____

Today _____/_____/_____

Today _____/_____/_____

Today ____/____/_____

Today _____/_____/_____

Today _____/_____/_____

Today _____/_____/_____

FAQ

As a supporter, coach and Alopecian, I've been asked so many different questions. I wanted to share some questions and my responses to those questions.

What is the cause of Alopecia?
It's and auto-immune deficiency where ones immune system mistakenly attacks the hair follicles because the immune system views the follicles as enemies thus hair loss begins. Usually when one has alopecia they also may have one or two other auto-immune disorders such as Allergies, Eczema, and or Psoriasis (please refer to www.aarda.org for additional information on the 63 known auto-immune disorders). Alopecia is unpredictable and usually presents itself when something life changing happens or stress may trigger it.

What is Alopecia Areata?
Round patches of hair loss

What is Alopecia Universalis?
Total body hair loss

What is Alopecia Totalis?
Complete hair loss only on the top of your head

What is Scarring Alopecia or Cicatricial?
This rare type of alopecia destroys the hair follicle permanently.

What is Traction Alopecia?
Caused by tension, tight ponytails or braids…I always say that this is the "self inflicted" alopecia

What is Androgenetic Alopecia?
Hereditary hair loss

What is Trichotillomania?
Hair pulling disorder

Are finger and toe nails affected?
Yes, since nails are of the same make up as hair, problems with your nails can occur.

Is it contagious?
No, alopecia is not contagious.

Will my hair grow back?

In some circumstances some do experience re-growth, however it is very unpredictable and one can not say for sure or guarantee. A cure or suitable treatment is still being researched and various methods of treatments are being used now.

Will my children get it since I have it?

It is highly unlikely, but is some cases a parent and a child can have alopecia. My daughter has alopecia areata, and she also has eczema which is another auto-immune deficiency. A doctor once told me that if one has one auto-immune then they could possibly have 2 to 3 more that may show up at different stages of your life.

What are the treatments for Alopecia?

Your physician may schedule frequent shots that may help stimulate your follicles to promote hair growth. A common treatment that I hear about normally from other Alopecians is the topical (i.e. cream, foam). Some people opt for the natural products, such as homemade essential oil recipes. The one best ever thing you can do for yourself is RESEARCH! Research every avenue because what's good for someone else may not be good for you. Everyone will respond to treatments differently, please remember that before you jump into something you may regret doing. Educate yourself and understand Alopecia first…that's the best treatment.

Is there any support out there?

There may be a support group in your area. There are also alopecia support communities online such as Alopecia World, Her Alopecia, National Alopecia Areata Foundation, Team Alopecia, and or the Children's Alopecia Project. Search on the web, keyword "Alopecia Support" to conduct your own search. (Note: the support groups named are suggestions ONLY, my personal favorites, and are not for endorsement purposes.)

What is the best way to tell someone you have alopecia?

There's never really a good way to tell someone, it will be hard because of fear that they may reject you. I would always start by asking, "have you ever hear of alopecia?" Many will say "no" and if that's the case I would inform them that it's hair loss, patches, etc. Usually some will say that they actually know someone with alopecia. Now there's your "in" to let them know that you have a condition called "alopecia" and hold your head up high when you say it.

Is my wig fake looking?

When you ask this question to someone, make sure that you truly trust this person. You would probably want to put a disclaimer out there too before you ask by saying "I will not feel bad if you tell me the truth, that is why I'm asking you…so please tell me your true opinion". Some people will hold back from telling you the truth because they fear that your feelings may get hurt. By letting them know up front that you won't get hurt or mad will prove beneficial to you.

Will I ever be "Normal" again?

"Normal" will only be defined by you. Whenever you can become comfortable in your own skin (with hair loss) will be the time you become "Normal".

Will this get worse after Alopecia Unversalis?

Since AU is complete body hair loss, you can't experience anymore hair loss. You may experience an additional auto-immune deficiency but it is unpredictable.

How do you prepare child with alopecia for the possibility that they may be an adult with alopecia?

Continue to educate them about alopecia so they can understand what's happening to them. Try not to be so hush, hush around them and others about their condition. They should be treated the same as if they had hair. It seems that when parents make such a huge deal out of it, then the child becomes more self conscience about their hair loss. If parents really take a step back and look at the situation you'll see that it's not about you. Parents seem to inflict their fears and their acts about alopecia onto their child, not realizing it until it's too late. Just be their for your child when they wish to talk about it and give them outlets such as a journal so they can write what they are feeling down on paper. Let them know that it's ok to feel whatever they may be feeling. Also, when you catch people staring have cards available explaining what it is that your child has and reference Alopecia websites for their educational purposes. By this you'll save yourself anxiety, stress and anger and teach your child how to handle certain situations as they get older. Give them a choice too when it comes to their head coverings. Parents want to automatically cover the head up or suggest this because of their feelings and fear. Again, it's not about you (parent).

How is it that I have no control over something that's happening to my body (i.e. if I gain weight I can loose it or if I'm sick I can take medication or if I get wrinkles I can get Botox)?

Because alopecia is not something that you caused…if you eat less and exercise you WILL loose the weight and if you spend less time in the sun then you might escape extra wrinkles however wrinkles are even hereditary. Alopecia is triggered from internal cues where your immune system is attacking by your hair follicles by "mistake". It's so unpredictable you really don't have time to prepare or control what's about to happen.

Why do people think you are vain for wanting to present yourself as you wish (Bald)?

I always think that some people think that it's out of the "Norm" and "how dare you come out and parade your bald head all over the place?" I think too that some people mistake self love, self awareness and confidence as being vain. They don't understand that you know what's going on with your body and have accepted it.

Why are the choices people make debated so hotly between even those dealing with this condition (no hair, patchy hair, scarfs, wigs - shouldn't acceptance of choice be ok)?
Simple, everyone is at different stages of metamorphosis so there are going to be different views on the topic. Also, alopecia is so misunderstood and is not a real familiar, high publicized disorder.

Why do doctors often blame the person with AA for having it (stating stress as the one and only contributor)?
Alopecia is so misunderstood. Sometimes they don't know what's really happening to you. Change in ones life usually triggers the dormant lying alopecia. That change is usually followed by stress.

What natural or complementary therapies are available for treating Alopecia?
Personally I've tried an essential oil blend and massage therapy to the scalp.

Will I get used to being bald?
This will be up to you. It depends on how much you want to grow from this adversity that life has placed in your life or how much and how long you want to stay the victim. Growth will come from time because you did loose a huge part of what you thought made you, you. As you grow though, you'll soon find out that you are still you even without hair.

Why is wrong for a person with Alopecia to not want to stand out
It's not wrong for those who don't want to draw attention. So what if you wear a wig or a head wrap, the goal here is to become more aware and accept you as a person with a difference.

Do you believe that as an African American it is easier to hide behind weaves than other races to disguise their hair loss?
It may be easier but definitely not better. Extensions may speed the process up just from the mere tension of the sewn or glued in hair tract. This goes for all races because African Americans aren't the only ones that where hair extensions.

Why is it so hard for people to accept a bald woman than it is to accept a bald man? Since this is so common why should we hide?
Society says so! Media says so! Make up ads say so! Hair ads say so! The commercial with the guy shaving "his" head says so! Plus men have role models such as actors, basketball players, TV personalities, dad, and Granddad. Women have women who play sick on TV or aliens. We should not have to hide. We have to start taking our self worth back and start changing the way society views a bald woman. So the next woman who looses her hair due to alopecia or cancer treatments can feel ok about their beautiful bald self.

Because this society is appearance oriented and I fear that I may face rejection…When will I ever get to the point of truly revealing myself to friends, family and even strangers and feel completely comfortable?

Whenever you start to reveal your true self to YOU! Once you accept you for who you are it won't matter what anyone else thinks about you because now you matter to you and that's all that matters!

Resources

List of my favorite links that I've found useful and resourceful

Alopecia/Hair Loss Resources and Support
www.locksoflove.org
www.naaf.org
www.teamalopecia.com
www.carfintl.org
www.AlopeciaAreataRegistry.org - Research Registry
www.americanhairloss.org
www.childrensalopeciaproject.org
www.niams.nih.gov/default.asp
www.americanhairloss.org

Support Communities
www.alopeciaworld.com
www.heralopecia.com
www.womenshairlossproject.com
www.baldgirlsdolunch.org
www.brotherhoodofbaldpeople.com

Cosmetics – Wigs – Head Coverings
www.hollycosmetics.com
www.headcovers.com
www.4women.com
www.amekor.com
www.nuhair.com
www.hatsscarvesandmore.com
www.stylishnoggins.com
www.hatswithheart.com
www.healingheadwear.com
www.peggyknight.com
www.amyspresence.com
www.fuller-hair.com
www.stampmefabulous.com

Products
www.alopecia-art.com - Accessories
www.komfykids.com – Therapeutic dolls
www.gillette.com – Razors
www.headblade.com - Razor
www.whatdoyouseedesigns.com – Tshirts
www.inkproductions.com – Screen Printing and Embroidery

For Inspiration
www.bbibby.org
www.crownedregal.com
www.baldisbeautiful.org
www.teamalopecia.com

Books
Princess Alopecia by Yaacov Peterseil and Avi Katz
I Love you More by Laura Duksta and Karen Keesler
Bald as a Bean by Nancy Parsons
The Girl With No Hair: A Story about Alopecia Areatam by Elizabeth Murphy-Melas and Alex Hernandez
Because of Anya by Margaret Peterson Haddix
If Your Hair Falls Out, Keep Dancing! By LeslieAnn Butler

Resources Disclaimer
I am providing these suggested links and references as a resource ONLY, not as an endorsement. I took every effort to ensure the accuracy of the information provided, but I do not warrant the accuracy of any such information. It will be the reader's responsibility to contact any of the vendors listed in this book to determine whether the products it provides are appropriate for you.

Photographer Credits

Alopecians	Photographer
Julia Crittendon	Tristan Richardson, Studio Effects Radcliff, Kentucky
Shannon Cox	Amy Shaw, Expressions Photography Salt Lake City, Utah
Yolonda Johnson	Blair Rendro, Velvet Lens Atlanta, Georgia
Daria Rowe	Keith Rowe Husband
Mandy Grimm	Laurie Ryan Mom
Louise MacNeil Howell	Louise Vessey, Photos by Louise Vessey www.lightandvision.com
Holly Oyler	Tristan Richardson, Studio Effects Radcliff, Kentucky
Charmaine Findley	Tristan Richardson, Studio Effects Radcliff, Kentucky
Tamara Cramer Bornemann	Jeanne Kuiper The Netherlands
Yvonne King	Bruce Talbot Tempe, Arizona
Char Hartman	Jennifer Eidt Clyde, Ohio
Yokasta Martinez	Marlon Gentry, Marlon's Vision Photography Cordova, Tennessee
Anna Fitzpatrick	Aaron K (Black and White) Auckland, New Zealand

Alopecians	Photographer
Annette Moore	Daniela Sessa (Red Dress) Philadelphia, Pennsylvania
	Christine Moore Philadelphia, Pennsylvania
Dotty Jenkins	Southwest News Service United Kingdom
Andrea Roussel	Julia Crittendon Louisville, Kentucky
Jill Cook	Tristan Richardson, Studio Effects Radcliff, Kentucky
Carol Jones	Personal
Jenn Pendergrast	Tammy Taylor Photography
Catharina Wiberg	Personal
Katrina Brewer	Roxann Brewer, Timeless Memories Photography by Roxann Clinton, Maryland
Kiah	Julia Crittendon Louisville, Kentucky
Anthea	Personal
Demeiah	Julia Crittendon Louisville, Kentucky
Midori	Julia Crittendon Louisville, Kentucky
Scotlyn	Julia Crittendon Louisville, Kentucky

 # Special Thanks...

To Warner/Chappell for the use of India Arie's lyrics "I am not my hair" and to India Arie for her Light!

The words in this song have empowered me! This song came out during one of my remissions and it soaked in so much that even at the thought of loosing my hair again...I knew that it would be okay.

I was able to look in the mirror and affirm that I AM the soul that lives within and will always be no matter what!

Thank you!

"Sometimes it's hard and often I question Life's motives...I'm just glad that I'm choosing to Embrace Change"